CW01496856

Patient Parenting

Effective Anger Management for Parents to Help You Keep Your Cool When Your Kids Are Acting Up

Kara Lawrence

© Copyright 2021 - All rights reserved.

The content contained within this book may not be reproduced, duplicated or transmitted without direct written permission from the author or the publisher.

Under no circumstances will any blame or legal responsibility be held against the publisher, or author, for any damages, reparation, or monetary loss due to the information contained within this book, either directly or indirectly.

Legal Notice:

This book is copyright protected. It is only for personal use. You cannot amend, distribute, sell, use, quote or paraphrase any part, or the content within this book, without the consent of the author or publisher.

Disclaimer Notice:

Please note the information contained within this document is for educational and entertainment purposes only. All effort has been executed to present accurate, up to date, reliable, complete information. No warranties of any kind are declared or implied. Readers acknowledge that the author is not engaged in the rendering of legal, financial, medical or professional advice. The content within this book has been derived from various sources. Please consult a licensed professional before attempting any techniques outlined in this book.

By reading this document, the reader agrees that under no circumstances is the author responsible for any losses, direct or indirect, that are incurred as a result of the use of the information contained within this document, including, but not limited to, errors, omissions, or inaccuracies.

Table of Contents

Introduction

It's that moment when the teen doesn't listen.

You're doing a lot of talking, but it doesn't seem like your teenager is doing a lot of listening. It's starting to feel like you're selling a lifestyle to your teen that's the opposite of their desires! You're slowly becoming the drill sergeant in their life. You're repeating the same command (sometimes in the language of shouting) day after day, and when you think they've heard you loud and clear, it turns out they found a cleverer way to work around that command.

This is the part we never thought of before having kids. Or maybe we did? I used to have such a meticulous strategy that included all the mishaps I pictured may happen. I imagined what my response would be based on what worked (and didn't work) with my own parents. I even took notes of my friends raising their kids. Whenever I overheard a dilemma, I would think to myself, "Well maybe if she listened to her daughter more, she would've gotten the truth," or "they should've started early with that habit."

I knew raising a teenager wouldn't be the easiest thing but I wasn't unprepared.

But that's when reality strikes.

I'm standing in the kitchen, catching a couple of breaths before every sentence because my daughter is so boldly staring at me as if she had nothing to do with the three Ds in her classes, staying out late last night and rolling her eyes five times during this whole talk.

You're probably thinking this situation is the worst of the worst but fear not! You are not alone in your difficulties.

There is a way to communicate to your teen and actually be heard. The key word is 'communication' and to be 'heard.' These words require the utmost imperative principle in the world of parenting: Patience.

Yes, it's easier said than done, but very possible with step-by-step guidance! You'll know the difference between things like:

- Talking to vs. talking at
- Listening vs. waiting for the speaker to finish talking
- Reacting vs. responding

If you're a parent, or soon-t0-be parent, patient parenting takes practice. Don't for a second believe it's too late to start. It's never too late to reach your teenager. May be hard to believe, but they want to get along with you. You're on two different pages right now but that doesn't mean your child doesn't want you in their life.

Take the opportunity to strengthen your relationship with your teen(s).

Chapter 1:

Patient Parenting

It's that thing we know we need to practice but wouldn't mind a little reminder from time to time. Patience. When your son or daughter was a toddler and they ignored your "Please don't touch that" request for the third time, patience took a giant leap out the window.

Yet still, the majority of parents express a wish to become more patient with their children (Rowden, 2021).

What is patience, exactly? Is it tolerating bad behavior? Is it turning the other way, pretending not to see it? Many people, including myself, believe that patience involves keeping cool in the face of a child's excessive acting out behavior. Don't underestimate the power of a passive reaction.

It entails keeping your emotions under control so that you can answer wisely and efficiently rather than shouting, swearing, or saying things you may later come to regret.

Honestly, however, is it really possible to be so patient in the first place? I mean, it's conceivable that it will happen at some point, but is it a realistic goal?

Look at some of the usual circumstances in which parents wish they could be more patient with their children:

It is the hundredth time that your daughter begs for something that you have previously denied her, prompting you to exclaim an emphatic 'NO!' that can be heard throughout the house.

You ask your kid to pick up his dirty dishes (again, for the umpteenth time) and find yourself speaking in a tone that betrays any sense of calm or composure you may be attempting to convey.

When you wake up Monday morning, the last thing you want to do is rush to get yourself and everyone else ready to go to work on time.

You've just returned home after a hard day at work. As you struggle to get supper on the table, you're simultaneously mediating a fight between two of your children and assisting another with his homework.

Parenting is difficult, and the scenarios described above are unavoidable. When it comes to parenting, there will always be challenges. Following on from that thought, here are four things you may do to improve your capacity to be patient.

What is Patient Parenting?

First, we need to understand what it means to be a patient person. No one can turn on patience like a light switch. It must be within us if we're going to do one of the hardest jobs on the planet (yes, parenting is way up there).

When it comes to virtues, patience is a quiet one. It is a shift in way of life that will provide a plethora of advantages (I will go further into them a bit later).

It's often shown behind closed doors rather than on a public stage: a parent reading his third bedtime tale to his children, a dancer waiting for her injury to heal, and so on. Impatient people are the ones that draw our attention in public: vehicles honking in traffic, disgruntled consumers waiting in long queues. A movie on patience would be a bit of a snoozer, but we have epic movies extolling the qualities of bravery and compassion, so why not make one about patience?

However, patience is crucial in everyday life—and it may even be the key to living a happy existence. Because patience is defined as the ability to remain calm in the face of irritation or hardship, we may practice it almost anywhere there is frustration or adversity, which is to say, almost everywhere. The ability to maintain tolerance can be the difference between irritation and serenity, being concerned and relaxed, whether at home with our children, at work with our colleagues, or at the grocery store with half of our city's population.

Throughout history, religions and philosophers have extolled the virtue of patience; now, scholars are beginning to do the same. Recent studies have shown that, indeed, good things do come to those who are patient and patiently wait. Some of these scientifically proven advantages are discussed in further detail here, along with three suggestions for cultivating more patience in your life.

It seems that there are common methods for developing patience as well. According to recent patience study, the following are some recommended strategies:

- Change the way you think about the circumstance. It is not just an involuntary emotional reaction that makes you feel impatient; it is also a result of your cognitive ideas and beliefs. If a coworker is late to a meeting, you may either be upset about their lack of respect or take advantage of the additional 15 minutes to catch up on some reading. Because patience is associated with self-control, actively attempting to moderate our emotions may aid in the development of our self-control muscles.

- Make use of mindfulness techniques. A six-month mindfulness program in school was shown to reduce impulsivity and increase the willingness to wait for a reward in one study of children. Christine Carter, of the Greater Good Science Center, also encourages mindfulness practice for parents: You may react with greater patience if you take a deep breath and acknowledge your emotions of rage or frustration (for example, when your children start yet another dispute just before night).

- Gratitude should be practiced. According to another research, persons who were feeling thankful were also better at postponing gratification for a longer period of time. When offered the option of receiving an immediate monetary reward or waiting a year for a greater ($100) windfall, participants who were less thankful opted for the quick payment option after the immediate payment offer reached $18. People who were grateful, on the other hand, may hold out until the number reaches $30. Having gratitude for what we have now does not imply that we are yearning for additional possessions or better situations right away.

However, although we may attempt to protect ourselves from irritation and difficulty, these feelings are unavoidable aspects of being human. Exercising patience in ordinary circumstances, such as dealing with our punctuality-challenged colleague, may not only make life more pleasant in the now, but it may also pave the way for a more rewarding and prosperous future.

1. People who are patient have greater mental health.

The following finding is probably easier to accept if you think of the stereotypically impatient individual in your mind: Face flushed, steam rising from the top of the head. Sure enough, a 2007 study by Fuller Theological Seminary professor Sarah A. Schnitker and University of California, Davis psychology professor Robert Emmons found that patients tend to experience less depression and negative emotions, perhaps because they are better able to cope with upsetting or stressful situations (Newman, 2016). They also describe themselves as more thoughtful and grateful, as well as feeling a stronger sense of connectedness to humanity and the cosmos, as well as a larger sense of affluence.

According to Schnitker, in 2012, we should deepen our concept of patience, acknowledging that it comes in a variety of colors and patterns (Newman, 2016). One sort of patience is interpersonal patience, which does not include waiting but rather involves being calm in the face of aggravating individuals. In a research of over 400 students, she discovered that individuals who are more patient with others are also more optimistic and content with their life as a result.

Another sort of patience is the ability to endure life's difficulties without becoming frustrated or depressed;

for example, consider the jobless person who continuously fills out job applications or the cancer patient who waits for her treatment to begin to work. Surprisingly, in Schnitker's research, this form of brave waiting was shown to be associated with higher levels of hope.

Finally, research seems that having patience while dealing with everyday difficulties such as traffic jams, lengthy queues at the grocery store, or a malfunctioning computer is associated with excellent mental health. People who have this form of patience, in particular, are more content with their lives and experience less depression.

The findings of this research are encouraging for persons who are already patient; but, what about those of us who desire to become more patient? When Schnitker conducted research in 2012, she asked 71 students to take part in two weeks of patience training, during which they learned how to recognize feelings and triggers, manage their emotions, empathize with others, and meditate, among other things. Participants reported feeling more tolerant with the difficult persons in their life after two weeks, as well as feeling less sad and having greater levels of pleasant emotions after two weeks. In other words, patience seems to be a talent that can be developed over time (more on this below) and doing so may have positive effects on your mental health.

2. People who are patient make better friends and neighbors.

When it comes to interpersonal interactions, patience may be considered a sort of compassion. Consider your closest friend, who consoles you night after night through the agony that simply won't go away, or your granddaughter, who grins through the narrative she has heard her grandpa tell countless times, and you will understand what I mean. Indeed, research reveals that individuals who are patient are more cooperative, more empathetic, more egalitarian, and more forgiving than those who are not patient. When it comes to patience, Debra R. Comer and Leslie E. Sekerka wrote in their 2014 research that it involves firmly taking some personal anguish in order to relieve the suffering of others around us (Newman, 2016).

Evidence of this may be found in a 2008 research in which participants were divided into groups of four and asked to donate money to a common pot, which would then be doubled and shared among the participants. Participants were given a financial incentive to be frugal, but those who were patient were rewarded by contributing more to the pot than their fellow players.

It is possible to find this sort of selflessness in persons who have all three forms of patience indicated above, rather than only interpersonal patience: The personality attribute of 'agreeableness,' which is characterized by warmth, friendliness, and collaboration, was shown to be connected with all three in Schnitker's 2012 research.

Individuals who were interpersonally patient were also less lonely, probably because developing and maintaining friendships—with all of its eccentricities and blunders—generally needs a good deal of patience. Schnitker and Emmons stated in their 2007 research that patience may help individuals to endure imperfections in other people, therefore demonstrating greater generosity, compassion, mercy, and forgiveness (Newman, 2016).

On a collective level, patience may be considered to be one of the cornerstones of civil society. When it comes to voting, those who are patient are more inclined to do so, even if it means waiting months or years for our elected officials to adopt better policies. Our predecessors' survival, according to evolutionary theory, was made possible by their ability to conduct good things and wait for others to reciprocate rather than seeking instant payment (which would more likely lead to conflict than cooperation). In a similar line, patience is associated with confidence in the people and institutions in our immediate environment.

3. Patience is essential in achieving our objectives.

The road to success is a long one, and people who lack patience—those who want to see results right away—may not be ready to travel it. Consider the current criticisms leveled at millennials for their unwillingness to "pay their dues" at an entry-level job and for hopping from position to position rather than developing and mastering their craft.

In her 2012 research, Schnitker also looked at whether students who are patient are more likely to complete their tasks. In five questionnaires they completed over the course of a semester, patient individuals of all shades indicated that they put out more effort toward their objectives than other people did, according to the results. The individuals demonstrating interpersonal patience made greater progress toward their objectives and were happier when they attained them (especially if the goals were tough), when contrasted with the individuals demonstrating less interpersonal patience. According to Schnitker's study, the fact that these patient achievers were more satisfied with their achievements explained why they were more satisfied with their lives as a result of their achievements.

4. The virtue of patience is associated with good health.

Although the research of patience is still in its early stages, there is some growing evidence that it may even be beneficial to our health. In a 2007 research, Schnitker and Emmons discovered that patients were less likely to report health issues such as headaches, acne flare-ups, ulcers, diarrhea, and pneumonia than non-patients (control subjects). Other study has shown that persons who demonstrate impatience and irritation — two characteristics associated with the Type A personality — are more likely to suffer from health problems and have worse sleep. We might reasonably infer that if patience can help us cope with the stresses of everyday life, then it may also help us avoid the negative health consequences of stress.

Can Anyone Parent Patiently?

Because of reduced stress, you'll have better mental health. The ability to be patient is not often included as a good attribute on a resume, but it is undeniable that individuals who are patient are more enjoyable to be around, both at work and in their daily activities. A patient parent is someone who has learned how to be a patient person in general.

Don't feel like you're being singled out! A quality that virtually everyone could improve on is the ability to communicate effectively.

It's possible that outside of the family dynamic, you have encountered circumstances when you were accused of being impatient, or you are already recalling instances in your life where having patience may have resulted in a better work position or fewer disagreements with your friends and family. Everyone who is willing to make the following lifestyle modifications might consider experimenting with the patient parenting approach:

- **It's time to practice patience!**

Although it may seem obvious, exercising patience is a genuine technique to enhance your ability to tolerate difficult situations. After all, how does one go about honing one's piano-playing abilities? Alternatively, how about preparing the perfect poached egg? Practice, practice, and even more practice.

Everyday life will no sure present you with several chances to improve your patience, but if you want to maintain more concentration and control while practicing, consider the following suggestions:

- Read a challenging book, such as War and Peace, to test your skills.

- Put together a giant jigsaw puzzle or a book of Sudoku puzzles.

- Make a commitment to preparing meals from scratch.

- Take public transportation to and from work.

- While you're waiting for appointments, refrain from glancing at your phone.

- Offer to babysit for a friend or a member of your family.

All of these jobs need patience because they compel you to wait and push you to let go of expectations, both of which are essential for learning to be more patient.

- **Consider the reasons behind your impatience.**

Concentrating on the source of your impatience might assist you in shining a light on your impatience.

Waiting in line at the grocery store because you're hungry and want to go home to eat is something you despise doing, right? Or is it because you're running late for a meeting or an event?

Examine the true causes for your impatience and determine what they are. When you identify the causes behind your sentiments, you may be in a better position to gain control over them and avoid obsessing about them in the future.

- **Don't burn yourself out over short-term discomfort.**

Even though life is the longest thing any of us will ever do, there are moments when even a few minutes may seem like an eternity in comparison.

When you find yourself in one of these circumstances (such as being placed on hold or caught in traffic), it may be incredibly unpleasant. You are sitting in a waiting room with little to no influence over what is happening.

However, keep in mind that you are only feeling uncomfortable. These scenarios are neither impossible nor life-threatening, so even if they are not pleasant, they are tolerable in the long run. It is possible that learning to identify and accept pain may make it easier to deal with it later on.

- **Distract yourself from your work.**

Waiting is required in many circumstances that call for perseverance, such as a prolonged airline flight or a long queue at a restaurant.

In these situations, there is little you can do to make things go faster, but you may use that time wisely if you divert your attention away from the situation.

Make time to listen to a podcast, compose a brief email you've been wanting to send, get into crossword puzzles, or finally tackle that Duolingo foreign language course you've been wanting to do. There are a variety of activities that may be done to pass the time that do not include merely seething about the issue and feeling angry or unhappy.

- **Recognize the sources of your impatience.**

The lightbulb going out in your bathroom is likely to be little more than an inconvenience during the day.

The majority of us have similar triggers that cause us to feel impatient, and these triggers are often triggered by repeating occurrences. This might be anything from obnoxious neighbors who are up at all hours of the night to children who do not put their shoes away after school.

Recognizing these impatience-inducing cues might assist you in controlling your reactions. You may either find measures to relieve or prevent them (for example, by contacting your local council or rewarding youngsters who keep their rooms clean), or you can learn to understand that they will continue to occur and that being impatient will do nothing to assist the situation.

- **Become more empathic.**

When you are impatient with someone, chances are that they are the source of your frustration. In most circumstances, a little empathy may go a long way.

Consider the following scenario: you're trapped behind an old gentleman or lady in line at the grocery store, furious as you watch them carefully count out their cash and coins one by one.

This is the time for you to pause and remind yourself to be empathic rather than frustrated with others. If they are making you late, consider them to be your own elderly relatives, or even your own loved ones, who you are neglecting.

The simple act of remembering that the 'cause' of your frustration is most likely just human, and that they are most likely doing the best they can to accommodate you may make you feel much more patient in the present.

- **Engage in meditation and mindfulness exercises.**

When it comes to coping with nearly every unpleasant emotion, meditation and mindfulness are particularly helpful techniques, and they are especially good when it comes to dealing with impatience.

Generally speaking, mindfulness is believed to be a mental talent in which proponents pay close attention to the present moment, enabling them to be aware of their thoughts and emotions, as well as to be appreciative of the little things. A meditation session provides an opportunity to just breathe, feel the body relax, and concentrate on nothing more than the next breath. This may help to regain control of one's thoughts and shift the emphasis away from bad feelings.

In conjunction with one another, these two disciplines may provide a potent antidote to the stress of impatience, with several studies documenting their beneficial benefits on reducing blood pressure, lowering anxiety levels, and boosting blood circulation.

Meditation and mindfulness will be discussed in more depth later in this book.

- **Make a mental note of your impatience.**

Sometimes just admitting a harmful behavior might be enough to help you break it. Consider the way in which individuals employ "swear jars" to keep themselves from cursing. You may use the same kind of strategy to deal with your impatience.

Fill in the blanks of a notepad app on your phone or a paper notebook with every incident in which your impatience burst out of control.

You will be able to spot frequent patterns and triggers within a short period of time, as well as how much time you are squandering by being impatient. As a result of your calmed-down state, you may be able to look back on a scenario with more objectivity and see that your impatience was baseless, which may help you better prepare to cope with a similar circumstance in future.

- **Retrain or educate those who are causing you to be impatient.**

In certain circumstances, your impatience will be caused by the ineptitude, blunders, or inability to follow procedure on the part of another person. This is most common at work; however impatience may also come from spouses, friends, children, or businesses that you contract with for services.

Investing some time in retraining or instructing people involved may be sufficient to resolve the issue in these situations.

Whether it's a coworker who makes the same error over and over again, or a cleaning firm that cleans your home wrong every week, these are all problems that may be resolved with proper training and education.

Suppose you are becoming frustrated because your office assistant continues sending emails that are plagued with errors. You may get down with them and discuss how to remedy the problem. For example, you might walk them through the most frequent or humiliating misspellings, or you could assist them in installing a more accurate spellchecker.

It will need some time commitment now, but it should eliminate the source of your frustration in the long run.

- **Take some time off for yourself.**

Give yourself a break - both figuratively and practically.

Spend 10 minutes outdoors, take a brief stroll around the block, or just move away from the source of your frustration.

It is possible that taking a short pause may allow you to clear your mind and tackle the subject with problem-solving logic rather than harmful irritation.

- **Accept what you can't change and move on.**

Many circumstances in life need patience, and there are times when there is simply nothing you can do to change the situation.

Possibly, you're waiting to hear back from the bank, or you're waiting to recuperate from an injury so that you can go out and do some physical activity once again. These things just take time, and fretting over them does nothing to improve the issue—or you personally.

Recognize these occurrences and make an effort to accept them. Being stressed out by them will just make you feel worse but accepting that you can't alter the situation can free up your thoughts to focus on things that are better in your life.

Consider using a mantra in similar situations, something along the lines of, "This is completely out of my control, so I'm going to do all I can not to get stressed out." Saying things out loud might sometimes be beneficial in helping you absorb them more efficiently.

- **Keep your eye on the bigger picture.**

When you look back five years from now, will the source of your impatience still matter? Is it really going to matter in five hours?

Because the reason for your impatience is seldom the end of the world, you may be able to let it go more easily if you remind yourself that it is not interfering with the broader goal.

In the event that anything minor or inconsequential is driving you insane, attempt to put it into perspective with the rest of your life. Imagine this: if you're upset over being overcharged at the drive-through for a milkshake, ask yourself if the additional dollar or two will genuinely have a negative influence on your financial situation. If the answer is no, make every effort to keep your attention on the delicious treat rather than the unexpected expenditure.

- **Keep your eye on the prize.**

Remembering the aim, which is distinct from "thinking about the larger picture," is a technique for moving past impatience by having a particular cause in mind.

As an example, although sitting during a toddler's tantrum is never pleasant, the purpose you're doing it may be to educate them that shouting will not result in them receiving what they want. Alternatively, you may be putting up with a bad situation at work, certain that your endurance will place you in a strong position to be considered for advancement.

In any scenario, if you have a precise purpose for putting yourself through difficulty, keep your attention entirely on that reason rather than allowing yourself to get bogged down in the agony itself.

Finding healthy ways to deal with your impatience is number fifteen.

A valuable talent for anybody, and for any undesired sentiments, is the ability to find a healthy outlet for one's bad emotions.

Individuals might find relief via different types of exercise, such as jogging or yoga. Others can find relief through creative outlets, such as scrapbooking or writing, while others can find relief through constructive tasks, such as cooking or gardening.

Make a list of outlets for your frustrations and refer to them anytime you are feeling overwhelmed.

- **Look to others for help.**

Take a look at you to see how other individuals are coping with the same challenging issue.

There are numerous instances in which you are not alone in enduring difficult circumstances, and when you are surrounded by people, you have two alternatives for coping with the matter at hand.

In the first instance, you may benefit from the experiences of others. Keep an eye on how they handle things and try to replicate their calm demeanor in order to develop your own tolerance.

In the second, you have the opportunity to set the tone by setting an example. When you're ready to scream inside, having an audience on your side might allow you to keep your cool and put on a facade of stoicism and realism.

- **Keep in mind that you will not instantly become a patience guru.**

This may seem to be a little paradoxical, but patience with patience is a virtue.

Unsurprisingly, a guy who tries to run a marathon with no prior preparation will not make it very far. Acquiring to be more patient is no different from learning any other talent. It requires consistent practice to become proficient in any skill.

Recognize that you will make errors, grow irritated, and experience difficulties. Understand that one week of experimenting with different ways to become more patient will not miraculously change you. Making a habit takes time, and the only way to succeed is to just keep trying until you succeed.

- **Give yourself permission to be impatient—everyone gets impatient at times.**

When anything happens in life that is too difficult, too infuriating, or too disappointing to simply take a deep breath and go on, it is called a "life event." You may allow yourself to be impatient within this little window of opportunity.

Making a promise to yourself that you'll never be impatient again is analogous to making a promise to yourself that you'll never eat another french fry. And just like with a rigid diet, allowing yourself to indulge every now and again might be beneficial in flushing out these unwanted cravings.

As long as you are not endangering anyone's safety, expressing your annoyance to a friend, punching a pillow, or going someplace alone to let out a releasing scream may all help you get over your impatience more quickly, even if you are partially caving into your feelings of impatience.

Having the knowledge that you can store your frustration for situations when it is actually warranted may help you be more patient the rest of the time.

- **Concentrate on the small victories.**

Certain procedures might take a long time, and it can seem as if you are making no progress despite your efforts in certain instances.

Although this is the case, there are likely to be modest - even microscopic - victories along the road in these situations. Pay attention to the little things that go well to remind yourself that you are making progress, even if it is at a snail's pace.

An excellent example is the purchase of a house. This process starts with a seemingly infinite number of open houses, followed by conversations with a plethora of real estate agents, comparisons of financing alternatives, and consideration of the advantages and disadvantages of different suburbs, and that's just the beginning. The procedure is one that requires patience, but with each choice taken and each piece of paper signed, you get closer to your eventual destination. Celebrating those minor victories as distinct milestones on the path to success is important.

- **De-stress in other areas of your life.**

Losing patience is a symptom that occurs rather often. You may be exhausted, agitated, or otherwise depressed, which creates an environment in which even the smallest complaint might seem like the most insurmountable obstacle.

Instead of concentrating your efforts on keeping your cool in stressful circumstances, use your resources into de-stressing in other aspects of your life. This might signify one of the following:

- Taking on less responsibility

- Increasing the number of jobs delegated

- Taking some personal time is important

- Setting sleep as a top priority

- Making a reservation for a vacation

However, if you choose to lessen your daily stress, you may find it simpler to increase your patience if you eliminate the underlying cause of your impatience.

- **Take pride in your ability to be patient.**

It is possible to feel proud of your patience when you believe it to be a talent, similar to baking or piano playing.

When you take pleasure in your ability to be patient, you will begin to perceive yourself as someone who is skilled at being patient. Seeing yourself as patient may help you become more patient more quickly in this situation - faking it till you make it can help you become more patient more quickly.

In a stressful situation, this self-reminder might assist you in maintaining your calm and exuding nothing but patience.

- **Seek assistance from others.**

Finally, if the situation is one that you are unable to better, you may be able to enlist the assistance of others in the process.

Take, for example, the situation when you are trying to complete a report at work because other team members are not giving their fair part. Discuss the problem with top management and seek assistance in ensuring that your team members fulfill their responsibilities before you lose your patience with everyone.

As a result, losing patience is nearly never an isolated event, and since other people are almost always involved, there will almost always be a chance to reach out.

- **Patience doesn't mean tolerance.**

Learning patience for the sake of your teenager (and your mental health) is imperative.

Remember, despite all of the ways you may learn to be more patient, you must constantly maintain in the back of your mind the notion that you are not required to be patient all of the time. In situations outside of family dynamics, maintaining a stoic demeanor might be more harmful than tackling a problem full on.

For example, your supervisor may be delaying the payment of a raise you were promised, or a spouse may be behaving badly and expecting you to be nothing but patient with them.

In such situations, remember your own self-worth and don't put your own well-being ahead of your own patience (and this will prove to be a great lesson to pass down to your teenager).

Overall, patience is as valuable as the proverbial virtue it is said to be, if not more so. Teaching yourself how to be more patient may be good to your health, your career, and your relationships, and it is possible that you will be able to add this really valuable talent to your resume as a result of your efforts.

Benefits of Patient Parenting

Children imitate what they see, and when you parent with patience, you demonstrate respect, empathy, security, and positive self-esteem to your children. These are the attributes that you wish to instill in your kid as he or she grows. The experiences that teach your kid how to be present and personal, not just with himself, but also with others, are the ones that matter the most.

As a result, when you "Stop, Look, and Listen" to your kid, you demonstrate to him that he is important, that you believe in him, and that you are sensitive to and compassionate toward his emotions. Active listening is built on patience and leads to the self-confidence that is necessary for self-mastery to take place. Finally, patience fosters not just empathy and compassion, but also confidence and competence in the person who has it.

Children are social learners who learn via experience, exposure to a variety of environments, role modeling, and imitation (Cross, 2016). Be the change you want to see in the world. As a result, you will be more present in your child's life, as well as in your own. When you converse with your kid, paying attention, being an active listener, and keeping eye contact with him, you may reduce his irritation and send him the message that you are with him and there for whatever he is doing at the time. This teaches him that patience means really listening to others and being present in a given situation.

Repercussions of Losing Your Temper

Yes, you had a legitimate cause for yelling. Your youngster will come up with a zillion reasons why you should give them a good earful. However, losing your cool with your kid produces a more serious issue than you may imagine, as you will see below.

The fact is, shouting is never pleasant for anybody involved. Remember the last time someone or you screamed at each other and felt better as a result of your exchange? You went away from the dispute full of fury and may have excused your actions by pointing to their misbehavior as an example. Do you, on the other hand, have a positive attitude toward it? If you're still enraged, it's possible that something is wrong with you. In a two-year study, researchers discovered that the consequences of severe physical and verbal punishment on children were shockingly comparable. Yelling at children may be just as destructive as beating them, according to the findings (Sturiale, 2015). When a youngster is screamed at, he or she is more likely to engage in bad conduct, which results in even more shouting. It's a vicious circle.

If you're a parent who regularly screams at your children, consider if any of the following reasons apply to you:

I shout at my children because they don't listen. According to Joseph Shrand, Ph.D., an instructor of psychiatry at Harvard Medical School and author of *Outsmarting Anger: 7 Strategies for Defusing Our Most Dangerous Emotion* (Harvard University Press), as soon as you begin to raise your voice, you stimulate their limbic system which is an ancient region of the brain that is responsible for a variety of functions, including the fight-or-flight reaction. Your children may react in ways that are the polar opposite of what you expect, such as freezing up, fighting back, or fleeing. Examine the distinction between sending a request and communicating a command to see if you can detect a difference.

However, yelling is the only way I can get the respect of my children. Although it may seem like yelling garners respect, it really causes more damage than good in most cases. When you say something like that to another human being, Shrand explains that you're effectively saying, "You have no worth to me." And a human person, in their heart of hearts, just wants to be appreciated by another human being.

Hey, if I don't shout, they won't take my words seriously either! Because screaming instills fear rather than respect, yelling at your kid may really be considered a kind of bullying. Consider using Shrand's "Stop, Look, and Listen" strategy, which is as follows: Stop what you're doing right now. Make direct eye contact with your children to demonstrate that they are important. Then pay attention to what they're saying, speaking with them rather than at them. According to him, "It's a lot more fun to discover who your child is than it is to attempt to shape them into the person you want them to be."

But... I just can't help myself! I just lose my cool from time to time. You have some control over it, however. Do you still not trust me? Consider the following: If you were in the midst of yelling at your children and someone you truly respected came knocking on your door (your employer, the president of your co-op board, Michelle Obama), wouldn't you quickly put an end to the yelling? Blown horns make children feel alienated, undervalued, and distanced from adults. Instead, take a deep breath and think about what you would want to see happen in your life. Approaching the matter from a more level-headed perspective can provide greater outcomes while minimizing emotional harm.

I don't have the luxury of time to argue with them. Having a conversation with children does not take any more (or less) time than shouting at them. Maintaining our composure conserves energy, allowing us to use our emotional energies to collaborate rather than compete with our children.

In the meantime, though, I may slap them if I don't shout. Shrand says that it's crucial for parents who have struck their children to take a step back and see that the only way to get anybody to accomplish anything is through respect and conversation. Whenever someone has a positive feeling about you, they will want to help you in ways that you would never be able to coerce them into doing otherwise.

However, the harm has already been done, I've been shrieking for years! The brain is wonderfully fluid (Cross, 2016). In other words, it's developing, it's changing, it's forming new connections... This is referred to as 'neuroplasticity.' To put it another way, it's never too late to make a change in your approach. Keep in mind that showing your children respect might help them regain their feeling of self-worth. "Can you recall the last time you were enraged with someone who was treating you with dignity?" Shrand inquires. "Respect breeds trust, and trust enables us all to realize our full human potential."

Chapter 2:

Understanding Your Kids

Understanding your kid is one of the most essential things you can learn as a parent, yet it is one of the most difficult. It is really beneficial in learning how to be successful in guiding and caring for your kid as they develop and grow.

It is important to remember that your kid has a distinct personality attribute that will stay constant throughout his or her life. Observing your kid when they sleep, eat, or play is one of the most effective methods to get a better understanding of them (Myers, 2021). Look for characteristics that are constant. What kinds of activities do they like the most? Is it simple for them to adapt to new situations, or do they need more time to grow used to these new circumstances? These are typical traits of children, and your kid may exhibit some of these qualities as well. As much as possible, make time to chat to your children since this is critical to their ability to learn and comprehend new knowledge. When it comes to young children, less verbal communication is required and more facial expression and body language are required in order to grasp their ideas and emotions. By asking them questions, you will provide them the opportunity to express their sentiments to you.

For example, rather than asking them what they did at school, you may ask them what they made with their blocks today instead of yesterday. Instead of asking them whether they played with their playmate, ask them about the game they played with their buddy. Observing your kid's surroundings in order to learn more about a certain behavior that you have witnessed is another method of knowing your child. Relatives, childcare providers, friends, teachers, the neighborhood, the home environment, and other factors of your kid's surroundings may all have a significant impact on his or her behavior and development. Example: If your kid is acting aggressively toward other children at school, you may want to investigate all of the potential causes of their hostile conduct. Consider the possibility that they are associated with another youngster who is also displaying aggressive tendencies. Another probable root of such conduct might be one's immediate surroundings at home. Have there been any disagreements or fights at home recently that your youngster saw or heard about? What is the situation in the community?

When attempting to determine the source of your child's aggressive conduct, you should examine the following factors. Additionally, by seeing other children of a similar age group to your kid, you may have a better understanding of your child. You may learn a lot about child development by reading our suggested books and browsing our website, which has many recommendations and in-depth information. It's important to remember that you went through the same phases as a kid, and that the conduct of children in the same stage would be more or less the same. The rate at which one progresses through each level, on the other hand, is entirely subjective. When you understand your child's developmental stage, you will be able to give them opportunities and toys that will aid in their development and prepare them for the next stage of their development. At the same time, you, as a parent, would be able to establish expectations and restrictions that your kid would find reasonable and understandable.

As you've already realized, the responsibility of being a responsible parent is difficult, especially in this day and age when parents spend more time working than they do with their children. Having quality time is tough to come by when you are attempting to split your time between your professional life and your family life. Parenthood is a difficult task for many individuals, which may be discouraging for new parents. Understanding your kid is one of the most effective ways to become a good parent in today's society.

Teenagers Get Overwhelmed

The adolescent years mark the beginning of the transition from childhood to adulthood. Teens often express a great desire to be self-sufficient. As a result, kids may struggle with the fact that they are still reliant on their parents. Furthermore, they may be feeling overwhelmed by the mental and physical changes that are taking place.

Teens may also be subjected to a variety of different pressures, such as the following:

- Making friends and fitting in at school are two of the most difficult tasks.

- Doing well in school and earning excellent marks are important goals.

- Performing very well in activities such as sports.

- Participating in the event as a member of the household.

- Working a part-time job is something I like doing.

- College or their next stage in life after high school is what they are preparing for.

- The adolescent years are crucial because they are the time when your kid establishes his or her uniqueness. Many parents are perplexed as to what they may do to assist their adolescent.

Keep in mind that your adolescent may engage in some kind of experimentation while attempting to identify themselves. In order to do this, they may need to alter their beliefs, thoughts, haircuts, or attire. This is standard operating procedure. You shouldn't be bothered about anything. Inappropriate or damaging conduct, on the other hand, may indicate the presence of a problem.

Some teenagers are at risk for engaging in a variety of self-destructive activities, including substance abuse. These teenagers often suffer from poor self-esteem and familial difficulties. They may experiment with drugs or alcohol, or they may engage in unprotected sexual activity (Family Doctor, 2018). Aside from depression and eating disorders, kids are also susceptible to other health problems. The following signs and symptoms may indicate that your kid is experiencing difficulties:

- Behavior that is agitated or restless.
- Weight loss or growth is possible.
- There has been a decline in grades.
- I'm having trouble focusing.
- Feelings of despondency that persist.
- Not caring about other people or things.
- There is a lack of motivation.
- Fatigue, a lack of energy, and a lack of enthusiasm in activities are all symptoms of chronic fatigue syndrome.
- Low self-esteem is a problem.
- I'm having trouble falling asleep.
- Getting into trouble with the law.

It goes without saying that pressure and stress may have a direct impact on one's mood, which may explain why so many specialists feel that it can contribute to depression. Is it any wonder, therefore, that almost one in every four young people will suffer depression by the age of 19 according to recent studies? Young people are increasingly injuring themselves in order to cope with emotions of sadness and worry, which is unfortunately becoming more common. In fact, according to a survey conducted by Young Minds, self-harm among young women and girls is increasing at an alarming pace (Family Doctor, 2018).

Identify Their Problems

There are numerous facets of contemporary life that might cause a kid or adolescent to feel stressed, nervous, or concerned, ranging from peer pressure to scholastic expectations to household chores. Our experts provide an overview of some of the most prevalent causes as well as suggestions on how to best manage a kid who is suffering stress or sadness.

Here are some stressful situations that may be affecting your child's behavior:

- **Classes and assignments.**

Many youngsters believe they are under intense pressure to do well in school. Some students find the teachings they have to study during the day – combined with the homework they have to do in the evening – to be daunting, and if a kid falls behind in his or her studies, this may cause stress. In many cases, this indicates that they do not have enough free time to play and decompress.

A new report by Childline revealed that the service provided more than 2,795 counseling sessions on exam stress between 2018 and 2019, with a third of those sessions taking place in April and May alone (CABA, 2020). Exams can put children and teenagers under increasing pressure, so much so that a recent report by Childline revealed that the service delivered more than 2,795 counseling sessions on exam stress between 2018 and 2019.

According to the research, the top worries for youngsters include not wanting to disappoint their parents, having too many responsibilities, and doing their hardest but still failing. It was also shown that stressing about completing tests was having a significant impact on young people's mental health, with some resorting to self-harm or having suicide thoughts.

Sometimes, teenagers may feel like their parents are already counting them out. Remember, if your child feels like you don't believe they're capable enough to succeed in school, they will not try at all.

- **Making new acquaintances and dealing with social pressure.**

If your kid is starting a new school, establishing friends may place a lot of strain on them. Those who have difficulty making friends are more prone to feel alone. When children quarrel and have a falling out with their peers, they might get anxious. Many youngsters feel under pressure to fit in, which might lead them to do things that they are not comfortable with or are uncertain about at the moment.

- **Bullying.**

It was discovered in ChildLine's annual evaluation that bullying was the most prevalent cause for young people to seek help from the organization's programs for children aged 11 and younger (CABA, 2020).

As a parent, there are some signs and symptoms that you may watch out for that may indicate that your kid is experiencing bullying issues. These are some examples:

1. Being distant, apprehensive, and lacking confidence are all symptoms of depression.

2. Not wanting to go to school because one is doing poorly in school (for instance, pretending to be ill).

3. Personal possessions have been misplaced (or personal belongings becoming damaged).

4. Not getting enough nutrition or sleep.

5. Having injuries that are not explained, such as bruises.

6. The events of the world.

These days, it's almost hard to keep youngsters away from upsetting news stories about things like war, natural catastrophes, and terrorist acts. A consequence of this is that some youngsters may be concerned about their own safety and the safety of their parents, family members, and friends.

- **Difficulties or changes in the family.**

Family troubles and changes to the usual, ranging from moving to a new place to parents' divorce, may be stressful for a kid or adolescent and lead them to become stressed.

What can you do to help?

I know it's much easier to get frustrated when your teen isn't listening, but we have to think about the possibility that they're overwhelmed. Teens don't always deal with that feeling in the healthiest way. They may hide that feeling with a strong resistance to your guidance. If you have reason to believe your kid is under a great deal of stress and anxiety and may be suffering, the following are some things you may do to assist them:

- *Make sure you have time for them.*

Even though all parents are busy these days, it's crucial to spend extra time with your children than you normally would if you suspect they are concerned about anything. Making yourself accessible for enjoyable activities or just being in the same room as them might help you connect with them. Engage them in conversation about their day and show an interest in the issues that are important to them. However, avoid pressuring children into discussing their concerns - they will open up when they feel safe discussing them with someone else.

- *Encourage good sleep habits.*

Children who get the appropriate amount of sleep and rest may grow more robust to stress. Depending on their age, children need varying amounts of sleep. Visit NHS Choices to find out how many hours of sleep your children require for each age group.

- *Provide them with nutritious meals.*

If you want to help your kid develop better coping abilities, a good diet is also important. Make an effort to ensure that kids get at least 5 servings of a variety of fruits and vegetables every day of the week (CABA, 2020). If your children are reluctant to eat fruits and vegetables, there are a variety of strategies you may use to convince them to include them in their diet.

- *Make stress a regular part of your life.*

It may be beneficial to remind your children that some amount of stress is totally normal in everyday life, and that everyone is affected by it and must learn to cope with it in different ways. Explaining that it's all right to feel what they're experiencing may help them get the confidence they need to control their stress levels more effectively. If it helps, try talking about occasions when you've been stressed and how you dealt with the situation at the time.

- *Continue to keep them busy.*

Physical activity may aid in the management of stress in both children and adults, so make sure your children receive enough exercise. Some other activities that you may attempt with them include relaxation methods and even something as simple as breathing techniques. Try to set a good example for your children by using these techniques to control your own stress levels. If they see you doing so, they are more likely to follow in your footsteps.

When They Seek Attention

This is totally natural behavior among children, who are always seeking their parents' attention and favor. It only becomes an issue when they need it all of the time and begin to misbehave when they are not provided with it. Some children are natural charmers who can get pity from their parents by inventing tragedies out of little issues, whilst others wail and stamp their feet in order to obtain what they want. As the days go by, this desire to be in the spotlight becomes stronger and may become a source of anxiety for the child's parents. There are a variety of compelling reasons why children act in the ways that they do. As a parent, you must first get an understanding of their attention-seeking behavior and then take the appropriate actions to address it. Here are a couple examples of how you can differentiate the 'troubled' and the "troubled-attention-seeker."

1. They are very dramatic. A melodramatic youngster often utilizes their emotions to control their parent's thoughts and feelings. In any setting, you may discover them responding excessively or with disproportionate intensity to the circumstances. For example, "they will claim that their instructor despises them" or "they need meals served on a certain color plate." In the event that their requirements are not met, they will start sobbing and flinging items all about the place.

2. They pose as unwell in order to get sympathy. Occasionally, children may pretend to be sick in order to keep their parents from going out and spending more time with them. You will observe that the majority of the time when you tell them that you are going out, they will start sobbing and complaining that their head or stomach hurts.

Chapter 3:

Setting Boundaries for

Yourself and Your Children

So how do you draw the line with your children and actually enforce the new way of healthy disciplining.

Teens often find themselves in tough circumstances with friends, dating partners, and others, in which they are unable to explain their needs or their ideals because they lack the necessary communication skills. Even when their instinct is telling them that someone is crossing a boundary with them, they may find it difficult to express how the scenario is making them feel uncomfortable in their own words. Consequently, parents must work with their children to set healthy boundaries with other people in their lives.

Although everyone's definition of boundaries is different, when they are implemented effectively, they may assist kids in setting limits with others in order to protect themselves. Setting boundaries helps kids to communicate with others about what is acceptable and unacceptable to them, which is vital for teen friendships and romantic relationships.

With certain adult figures in their life, such as a coach or a relative, it may even be important to set boundaries. Here are some suggestions for assisting your adolescent in setting limits.

What Are Boundaries?

Boundaries are restrictions that kids create in order to protect themselves from being mistreated, deceived, or taken advantage of in some manner. It is via the expression of self-worth that others may learn about your adolescence, what they value in life, and how they want to be treated by other people. Moreover, setting boundaries might help your kid generate space between him or her and other people when they need it.

Healthy boundaries are essential for the success of any relationship, whether it is platonic or passionate in nature. Teens benefit from the process of creating boundaries because it helps them realize how they feel and what their limitations are. It also forces them to speak openly and honestly about those emotions and restrictions.

"I am fine with following each other on social media, but I am not cool with exchanging passwords," says Love Is Respect, a non-profit group that works to prevent adolescent dating abuse. "I am comfortable kissing and holding hands, but not in public," says the organization.

What's the Point of Setting Boundaries?

Developing the ability to create boundaries, both physically and emotionally, is a vital aspect of growing up. Building polite, helpful, and healthy friendships and dating relationships is also vital for developing a positive self-image and being happy (Gordon, 2021).

Unfortunately, many teenagers have difficulty establishing boundaries with their friends and in their dating relationships, and when this occurs, they are more vulnerable to anything from toxic friendships to bullying and dating violence.

Of course, establishing limits is not always simple. A youngster is forced to assert themselves and set boundaries as a result of this unpleasant situation, which may be quite harmful. Furthermore, expressing limits with other people might result in tough talks or uncomfortable circumstances with the other person.

Although it is one of the most difficult things for kids to learn, it is one of the most vital. It is not only important to create boundaries with other people in order to keep your adolescent safe, but it is also important to preserve their mental health as well. 4 Being in an unhealthy relationship or suffering dating abuse may have a lot of negative implications for the individual involved.

It is important for your teenager to consider creating boundaries with persons that make them feel uncomfortable, disrespectful, or unworthy. Examples include phony friends, a dominating dating partner, or an adult who makes them feel worthless, unworthy, or undeserving. Allowing others to treat your child in an unhealthy manner not only results in bad relationships, but it may also have a negative influence on your teen's mental and emotional well-being.

How to Define Your Boundaries.

Teens, like adults, find themselves in a range of various situations in their romantic relationships. They may need to tell one friend that they are not comfortable discussing their schoolwork with them, and they may need to tell another that they are not comfortable gossiping about other people. Perhaps one of your friends is extremely dictatorial, while another steals money on a regular basis from you. These are all situations in which establishing boundaries might be beneficial.

Adolescents may even find themselves in circumstances where they must express their thoughts regarding sex or alcohol to others.

The idea is that your child will encounter a variety of scenarios throughout their life that will question their values and beliefs and understanding how to create boundaries will help them stay safe while being true to themselves. Here are some pointers on how to establish boundaries:

Help your teen recognize and express their emotions.

It is not as simple as it seems to learn to detect and name various types of emotions. It requires effort on your teen's part to take a step back and consider how they are feeling in any given circumstance. They may be aware that they are disturbed, but do they identify as angry, irritated, or depressed? The ability to identify how they are feeling is the first step in establishing healthy limits.

Instill confidence in your teen by teaching them to trust their instincts.

Instruct your adolescent on the importance of always following their instincts. If something doesn't feel quite right or right about a scenario, it almost certainly is. Regardless of what other people may think, they are not being theatrical or excessively sensitive at all. The key is that they must be true to themselves and not to what they believe others want them to be or look like.

Assist them in recognizing and avoiding unacceptable behaviors.

Teens can need assistance in defining what constitutes a good relationship or friendship. Talk to them on a regular basis about what forms a good friendship or dating relationship, as well as what constitutes respect in their eyes.

Teens are not unusual in accepting undesirable behaviors from others, but when they do, they are sacrificing their own sense of self-worth and value.

As a reminder, remind them that everyone deserves to be treated with kindness and respect, and that if someone is not treating them well, they may need to create some boundaries with that individual.

In addition, consider the significance of digital boundaries.

The majority of today's relationships have a digital component to them.

Discuss internet etiquette with your adolescent, as well as sexting and online dating abuse with them. Make sure kids understand how to keep safe on the internet, as well as how to create boundaries with others who do not share their values.

Provide them with key phrases that they may use to defuse tense situations.

Setting limits is difficult and requires a great deal of experience. Moreover, it is something that takes deliberation and decision-making on your part. Teens, as a result, need some fundamental terms that will buy them some time. Here are a few illustrations: "I'll think about it and come back to you," "Thank you, but no thanks." "I'm not comfortable with that," or "Let me chat to my folks about it and get back to you tomorrow."

In the heat of the moment, knowing a few sentences to say might help to protect them from being overwhelmed or succumbing to pressure from their peers, which can be dangerous.

Allow them to practice at their own convenience.

Creating healthy boundaries with another person is difficult, even for adults in certain cases. As a result, kids should practice in a secure atmosphere with people who they know will always love them no matter what they do.

Allow your kid to express his or her feelings by saying 'no' to some requests and setting personal limits. The consequences of this might include communicating with family members about the need for space at times and avoiding interacting with extended family when they have a major test coming up.

Encourage your adolescent to develop autonomy and independence at home by enabling them to express their thoughts and make choices on his or her own behalf.

Explain that friendships have their own set of restrictions.

Too many times, teenagers fall into the trap of feeling that they must be everything to all of their pals at the same time. Be sure to emphasize that every friendship is unique and will play a unique function in each person's life.

The ability to be a good friend does not need agreement on every single subject. In reality, having opposing viewpoints or views is what makes interpersonal interactions so exciting. Encourage your adolescent to be himself or herself and to form healthy connections.

Demonstrate effective boundary-setting abilities.

In order to teach your adolescent strong boundary-setting abilities, one of the most effective methods is to model the behavior in your own life. Examine your interactions with others and make any necessary adjustments. Setting boundaries with those who attempt to take advantage of you or who don't treat you properly sets a positive example for others to follow. If you haven't already, start establishing limits in your own life.

Describe the dangers of not establishing boundaries.

In situations when a friend or romantic partner crosses the line, it's often a lot simpler for a kid to just let things go or not say anything at all. However, failing to establish limits is harmful and may even put children in danger. Even if nothing significant occurs in the connection, failing to establish boundaries may result in animosity and the deterioration of the friendship.

Remind them to be considerate of others' personal boundaries.

It's just as crucial for your kid to respect other people's limits as it is for them to develop their own rules and regulations. Healthy relationships, on the other hand, are based on mutual respect and open communication throughout the partnership. Maintain communication and ensure that your adolescent understands that it is as vital to respect the limits of others as it is to request that they do the same for them.

How to Set Boundaries

Young individuals might be perplexed by the concept of limits at times. Despite the fact that they may comprehend the notion and value of setting limits with other people, they may not be aware of what those boundaries look like in real world situations. As a result, it is critical to discuss what defines a healthy border and what constitutes an unhealthy boundary. If necessary, you may want to call out areas where they are weak in boundaries.

Healthy boundaries are important.

Healthy boundaries keep your kid safe emotionally and physically while preventing him or her from attempting to dominate or manipulate others. They determine your teen's desires and requirements without interfering with the rights and requirements of another individual. Here are a few illustrations:

Communicating a desire to go cautiously in a love relationship, as well as ensuring that permission is at the center of every encounter and that they do not feel pressured to do more than they want, are all important steps.

The act of asking someone to stop from teasing them about a sensitive matter, and then punishing that person for doing so by limiting the amount of time they spend together is known as a polite request.

Informing a friend that they do not feel comfortable drinking and asking them to support their choice not to consume alcohol.

Advising a buddy who requests to borrow money on a regular basis and does not refund it that they will not be able to give them any more money until they pay back what they owe is a good idea.

A sibling has expressed their want for alone time and has been asked to respect this desire by not stepping into their room while the door is closed.

Inviting a love partner to show consideration for their time spent with other people by refraining from contacting or messaging them constantly while they are out with others.

Boundaries that are unhealthy or a lack of boundaries

When teenagers first learn about limits, they may go too far in establishing them or they may fail to establish any boundaries at all. Both options have the potential to be harmful.

In order to do so, it's critical to point out areas in which your kid may need to set some limits or even loosen up a little bit. Here are a few illustrations:

- People are being excluded from their lives on a total and utter basis, and they are not trusting anybody.

- Demanding that their friends or dating partners be there for them at all times is not a good idea.

- Believing that people are aware of their thoughts and feelings and that they should react appropriately.

- Giving in to friends or dating partners, even if it means going against their religious or philosophical beliefs.

- Going against one's own ideals or convictions in order to fit in, be liked, or satisfy others is a kind of deception.

- Allowing a love partner to make choices for them or lead their lives without ever standing up for themselves or challenging this behavior is a dangerous habit to get into.

- Spending time with friends or dating partners who are unkind or rude to them is not recommended.

Developing the ability to create limits is something that every young person should be able to achieve. Ideally, you want to speak to your children about how to create boundaries before things become too difficult in a friendship or romantic relationship.

Indeed, setting healthy limits is an important element of having a positive sense of one's own worth. Kids who have a strong sense of self-worth are aware of who they are, what they value, and how they want to be treated; and when someone crosses the line in some way— either by taking advantage of them, picking on them, or pressuring them to do something they don't want to do—they are aware that something isn't quite right in the relationship and know how to recognize it.

Showing your kid how to set boundaries when someone crosses a line with them is the most effective method of dealing with these situations. You will be laying the groundwork for strong connections with your children that will last far into adulthood as a result of your actions. Crossing these boundaries will result in losing trust. Without trust, your difficulties will never end.

Chapter 4:

Identify and Manage Your Triggers

A third morning spent listening to the instructor explain why your kid is slipping behind in his subjects. She failed to return home at the agreed-upon hour for the third night in a row. Another weekend spent trying to have a dialogue with them, and they look much more rebellious than the last time you saw them.

Anger is the first, and most normal, response to have.

We all claim to understand what fury is. Whatever form it takes, we've all experienced it: whether as a passing irritation or a full-blown wrath.

Anger is a fully natural and, in most cases, beneficial emotion experienced by humans. However, when it spirals out of control and becomes destructive, it may cause issues at work, in your personal relationships, and in the general quality of your life, among other things. It may also make you feel as though you're at the whim of an unanticipated and overpowering feeling, which can be frightening.

But how far have you gone with your children thus far in your life? After all, it may seem like the best approach to raise awareness or induce panic, but then you find yourself questioning why your 15-year-old has just lied four times in one night as if they are clueless of the wrath you would bring upon uncovering their falsehoods.

If you confront your anger and have an understanding of what it is and where it comes from, you will be better able to maintain control as life's obstacles become more intense. Knowing how to assert yourself means you won't have to deal with the frustration of having to keep your anger under control in order to avoid upsetting your kid.

The Nature of Anger

Anger has some specific characteristics.

Anger, according to Charles Spielberger, PhD, a psychologist who specializes in the study of anger, is an emotional state that ranges in intensity from moderate annoyance to tremendous wrath and rage (American Psychological Association, 2021). Because anger is accompanied by physiological and biological changes, it is important to understand how it works. When you are furious, your heart rate and blood pressure increase, as do the levels of your energy chemicals, adrenaline, and noradrenaline.

Anger may be triggered by a variety of circumstances, both external and internal. When you are furious, you may be upset with a particular person (such as a colleague or boss) or incident (such as a traffic congestion or flight cancellation), or you may be upset because you are worried or brooding about your own issues. Anger may also be triggered by memories of painful or enraging events that have occurred.

Expressing Your Anger

A violent response to anger is the most spontaneous and natural approach to express a person's feelings of rage. Angry sentiments and actions are a normal and adaptive reaction to dangers; they elicit strong, often violent feelings and behaviors, which enable us to fight and protect ourselves when we are attacked. As a result, a certain level of rage is vital for human existence.

But hey, we can't physically attack every person that causes us irritation or irritation.

Laws, societal standards (and you know, common sense) all impose boundaries on how far our rage can lead us when it comes to physical violence.

Angry emotions are dealt with by a number of conscious and unconscious mechanisms, which are discussed below. It is possible to express yourself in three ways: expressing, repressing, and soothing. Expressing your furious sentiments in an authoritative, rather than aggressive, manner is the healthiest method to deal with your emotions. In order to do this, you must learn how to communicate your demands clearly and how to have them satisfied without causing harm to others. The ability to be assertive does not imply being forceful or demanding; rather, it entails showing respect for yourself and others.

Anger may be contained and then transformed or diverted if it is channeled properly. This occurs when you keep your anger under control, stop thinking about it, and concentrate on something constructive. With anger management, the goal is to restrict or repress your anger and redirect it toward more productive conduct. It is possible for your anger to turn inward on yourself if you are not permitted to express it in public. This is a risk with this sort of reaction. Anger that is directed inside may result in hypertension, high blood pressure, and depression.

Anger that is not voiced might lead to other issues. Pathological displays of anger, such as passive-aggressive conduct (getting back at others indirectly, without telling them why, rather than addressing them directly) or a personality that seems persistently cynical and angry, might result as a result. People who are continually knocking people down, criticizing everything, and making cynical remarks haven't learned how to vent their anger in a productive manner. It should come as no surprise that they are unlikely to have many successful partnerships.

Finally, you will be able to relax on the inside. Managing your external conduct requires you to simultaneously manage your internal emotions, which is taking efforts to reduce your pulse rate, calm yourself down, and allow the sensations to fade.

Is it true that some people are more enraged than others?

Individuals may be 'hot-headed,' according to psychologist Jerry Deffenbacher, PhD, who specializes in anger management. According to Deffenbacher, some people are just more 'hot headed' than others; they can get furious more quickly and strongly than the ordinary person (American Psychological Association, 2005). There are also some who do not express their anger in overly dramatic ways, but who are chronically irritated and cranky as a result. It is not always the case that easily enraged individuals swear and hurl objects; they may also retreat socially, pout, or get physically unwell.

When it comes to being quickly enraged, people tend to have what some psychologists refer to as a poor tolerance for frustration, which simply means that they believe they should not be exposed to irritation, difficulty, or annoyance. They are unable to take things in stride, and they get especially enraged if the situation seems to be unfair, such as when they are reprimanded for a tiny error.

What is it about these folks that makes them behave in this manner? There are a lot of things. One possible explanation is genetic or physiological in nature: According to some research, certain infants are born irritable, sensitive, and easily enraged from birth, and these indications are evident from a very young age in these children. Another possibility is a sociocultural one. Our society has conditioned us to believe that it is OK to express worry, despair, or other unpleasant feelings but not rage; we have been taught that anger is inappropriate. Consequently, we do not learn how to deal with or channel our emotions in a productive manner.

In addition, research has shown that one's familial heritage has an impact. People who are quickly enraged are often raised in households that are disorganized, chaotic, and lacking in emotional communication skills.

What Are Your Triggers?

So, what exactly drives individuals to get enraged?

For our children, there are several frequent causes for rage, including losing your patience, feeling as if your views or efforts haven't been valued, and simply not being listened to. Other sources of anger include recollections of painful or enraging experiences, as well as concern about one's own personal difficulties.

Aside from that, you have your own set of anger triggers that are based on what you were taught to expect from yourself, others, and the environment. In addition, your personal background influences your emotions to rage. For example, if you weren't taught how to express your anger effectively, your frustrations can simmer and make you unpleasant, or they might build up until you have an angry outburst that makes you feel embarrassed.

You may be more prone to furious outbursts due to inherited inclinations, brain chemistry, or physical issues that are present at the time of your birth.

No one else has the power to stimulate the emotions of parents and children like they do. Even as adults, we have a tendency to be illogical in our interactions with our own parents. (Can you think of someone who has more ability to upset you and make you behave childish than your mother or father?)

In a similar vein, our children press our buttons exactly because they are our offspring. When psychologists talk about "ghosts in the nursery," they are referring to the fact that our children elicit strong memories of our own childhoods, and we react by subconsciously reliving those memories, which are carved like forgotten hieroglyphics deep inside our psyches. Children's anxieties and wrath may be quite strong, and they can even overpower us as adults. In certain cases, it might be quite difficult to put these spirits to rest.

When we are having to manage with anger, it is beneficial to be aware of all of this. In addition, we must be aware that parental rage may be damaging to young children, in part because it provides us with an incentive to keep our emotions under control.

What Happens When You Express That Rage?

Consider the possibility of your spouse or wife losing their cool and yelling at you. Put yourself in their shoes, and picture them three times your size, looming over you. Consider the possibility that you are fully reliant on that individual for your food, housing, safety, and protection. Consider them to be your principal source of affection, self-confidence, and knowledge about the world, and that you have no other place to turn for these things in your life. Take whatever emotions you've conjured up and multiply them by a factor of a thousand. That sounds a lot like what occurs inside your kid when you are upset with them.

Without a doubt, we all become frustrated with our children, and even angered at times. The task is to summon our maturity so that we can manage the expression of our anger and, as a result, reduce its detrimental influence on others around us.

Anger is frightening enough. Using derogatory language or engaging in other forms of verbal abuse against the kid has a greater impact on the parent's own well-being since the child is reliant on the parent for his or her very sense of self. In addition, children who are subjected to physical aggression, such as spanking, have been shown to experience long-term consequences that extend into every aspect of their adult life, including poorer intelligence, stormier relationships, and an increased probability of drug misuse and addiction.

You should be concerned if your small kid does not seem to be terrified of your anger. This may indicate that he or she has seen too much of it and has built defensive mechanisms to protect themselves — and you. This has the unintended outcome of creating a youngster who is less likely to desire to act in a way that pleases you and is more susceptible to the influences of his or her peers. That implies you'll have to undertake some minor repairs around the house. Our anger is nothing short of scary to our children, regardless of whether or not they express it — and the more often we get enraged, the more defensive they will become and, as a result, the less likely they are to express it.

Manage Your Anger?

How do you deal with your own rage, if at all?

Your kid will begin to appear like the enemy while you're in "fight or flight" mode since you're human. When we're enraged, our bodies are ready to take on the world. Our bodies are flooded with hormones and neurotransmitters. They tension your muscles, raise your heart rate, and speed up your respiration. At such moments, it's tough to remain cool, but we all know that slapping our kids isn't the solution we're looking for, as much as it would provide immediate comfort.

Anger is a powerful emotion, but the most essential thing is to avoid acting on it. As a parent, your instinct will be to take immediate action and teach your kid a lesson. That's just your rage speaking, however. In its mind, this is a life or death situation. Even if it is, it is nearly never the case. Your kid will learn from you in the future, and it will be a lesson you want to impart. He or she will not be leaving your side. She's in your neighborhood.

So, make a promise right now to never beat, curse, call your kid names, or administer any punishment when irrationally enraged. Why not try yelling? Never yell at your kids, that's a tantrum. Don't use words when you need to scream, since they will just make you angrier. Instead, scream in your automobile with the windows rolled up. Just yell!

It's a twofold benefit to your children if you discover constructive methods to cope with your anger: you not only avoid hurting them, but you also serve as a role model for them to follow. The way you respond when you're upset may teach your kid a lot about how to deal with difficult circumstances.

Will you instill in your kid the belief that only because something is possible, it is right? There are tantrums among parents, right? That's how grownups deal with disagreement, isn't it? If this is the case, they'll see it as a sign of their maturity.

It is possible to teach your kid that anger is a natural part of life, and that learning how to control it is an important element of maturation. Here are the steps.

First, keep in mind the limits. Assassinate them with rage.

In many cases, our children's misbehavior is the result of a lack of boundaries that are nagging on us. As soon as you feel upset, it's time to take action. Not yell, please. Take action in a constructive manner to stop the conduct that is bothering you from happening again.

Let them know you've had a stressful day and encourage them to be respectful and restrain themselves for the time being, so that you don't become annoyed by their natural joy.

You may need to stop what you're doing, reaffirm your expectations, and redirect your children if they're doing something that's becoming increasingly annoying, such as playing a game in which someone is likely to get hurt, stalling when you've asked them to do something, or arguing while you're on the phone.

Before you act, take a moment to calm yourself down.

You need a means to calm down when you're this angry. Stop, drop (your plan for a minute), and breathe will help you regain control of your body and mind. You may take a deep breath and utilize it as a stopwatch. It provides you the option of what you want to do. No, I don't think that's what I want to do.

Remind yourself that this isn't a crisis at this point in time. Your hands should feel loose and relaxed. Breathe in for 10 more seconds.

You may attempt to find a method to lighten the atmosphere by making light of the situation. A grin even if it's forced conveys the message to your nervous system that there is no emergency and helps you relax. Humming is a good way to produce noise. You may want to turn on some music and dance to help you release your wrath.

A 15-minute daily mindfulness practice while your children are at school or sleeping may help you develop the neurological ability to calm yourself in stressful situations. Every time you delay acting when you're furious, you're rewiring your brain in a way that will allow you to better regulate your emotions in the future.

People still follow the old advice of clobbering a pillow, but it's better if you do that type of unloading in private, since witnessing you clobber that pillow may be a little alarming for your kid. To him, the pillow represents his skull, and the picture of Crazy striking Mommy will be etched in his mind forever. At the very least, it's a risky tactic, since research says that striking anything — anything — signals to your body that this is an emergency and that you should remain in "fight or flight." So, although it may 'discharge' energy and exhaust you, it fails to address the sentiments that are fueling your anger and may even exacerbate it.

The emotions that lurk underneath the rage may be felt by taking a few deep breaths and learning to accept yourself when you're upset. Allow yourself to experience such emotions by paying attention to the physical sensations they elicit. Avoid reinforcing your feelings of stress by 'thinking' about them; instead, focus on your breathing and see the tightness in your body transform and go. The rage will dissipate with time.

Count to three.

Recognize that attempting to interfere in any situation when enraged is a bad idea. Instead, take a break and return when you're ready to focus. Stay as far away from your kid as possible to avoid the temptation to reach out and angrily touch him. If you can manage it, just state:

When I think about it, I'm too upset to speak about it. To calm myself down, I'm going to take a break.

Your kid cannot win if you go. It shows them how terrible the offense is, and it teaches them how to manage their impulses. Use this opportunity to de-stress rather than working yourself up into a frenzy about how correct you are this time.

Take a break in the bathroom and splash some water on your face as you take a deep breath. Your kid will follow you if they are young enough to feel abandoned if you leave. Even in adult relationships, this is commonplace.) (Just in case.)

Walk over to the kitchen sink and run the palms of your hands under the running water. Breathe deeply and chant a mantra that brings you back into a peaceful state, like one of these: "I'm here for you."

"It's not an emergency," he responds.

"Kids need love the most when they don't deserve it."

"He's behaving this way because he needs my aid dealing with his overwhelming emotions."

"Today, all I have is love."

Saying your slogan out loud is good. A fantastic role model for your children is to show them that huge emotions can be handled well. Be prepared for your youngster to start quoting your mantra when he's furious.

When you're angry, instead of acting on it, pay attention to it.

Anger, like all other emotions, comes as standard equipment for human beings. What we're ultimately accountable for is what we do with it. Even while anger may teach us great lessons, it is seldom a good idea to act on those lessons unless it is absolutely necessary to protect ourselves. Limiting our outbursts of rage and then using them as a diagnostic tool to figure out what's going wrong in our lives is the best method to deal with our feelings of frustration.

Even if it's only a simple matter of enforcing rules before things get out of hand, putting the kids to bed half an hour earlier, or doing a little relationship repair work with our child, the solution may be found in our parenting. We may be astonished to discover that our anger is really directed at our spouse who isn't behaving as a full partner in parenting, or even our employer.

Counseling or a support group for parents may be necessary in certain cases, since we're carrying around a lot of unresolved anger that spills over into our children.

Make sure you are aware of the dangers of 'expressing' your anger to others.

Despite the widespread belief that we must 'vent' our anger in order to keep it from controlling us, expressing anger 'against' another person accomplishes nothing. In fact, studies have shown that the act of expressing one's anger only serves to exacerbate one's feelings of rage. As a result, the other person becomes more irate and resentful as a result of this. It's no surprise that instead of healing the divide, this further widens it.

Even more so, expressing one's rage isn't a true expression of one's feelings. As a result of your internal turmoil, you lash out at the person you're furious with. Expressing the pain or anxiety that's fueling your rage is the only way to be really honest, and you can do it with a partner. Your responsibility as a parent is to keep yourself in check, not to burden your kid with your feelings.

The first step is to take a deep breath and settle down. Before making judgments on what to say or do, think about what the 'message' of the anger is.

Be patient before enforcing punishment.

Don't do anything while you're irrationally enraged. Issuing orders on the spot is not required. As simple as saying, for example:

"The fact that you beat your brother after we've spoken about the pain of being hit is shocking to me. We'll chat about it later this afternoon after I've had some time to reflect about it. While I'm away, I want you to behave well."

Calm yourself down for 10 minutes. Don't relive the scenario over and over in your head; this will just make you more enraged. When you're stressed, apply the methods above to calm down. Don't be afraid to postpone the conversation if you've taken an additional 10 minutes to calm down and still aren't able to communicate effectively:

"As soon as I've digested what just transpired, I will come back and discuss it with you. My supper prep and your schoolwork must take precedence at this moment."

Take a few minutes after supper to sit down with your youngster and if required, lay down some boundaries. He may be able to hear your side of the story, and you'll be able to react with fair and enforceable restrictions to his actions.

Avoid using physical force at any costs.

More than eighty-five percent of teenagers report that they have been spanked or slapped by a parent (Journal of Psychopathology, 2007). Research shows that physical punishment such as spanking has a long-term harmful influence on children's development. It is highly discouraged by the American Academy of Pediatrics.

It's a wonder whether the rise in anxiety and sadness among adults in our society is at least in part due to the effect of growing up in a world where so many of us were harmed by adults. There is a tendency for parents who have experienced physical abuse to downplay their experiences because of the intense emotional distress that comes with such a disclosure. Repressing our childhood trauma just makes us more inclined to abuse our own children in the future.

Slapping your kid may make you feel better for a short period of time, but it is detrimental to your child and sabotages all of your excellent parenting efforts. As a result of spanking and slapping, things might escalate. Spanking may even be addicting for parents since it allows them to let out their frustrations and relieve their stress. Fortunately for you, there are alternatives that won't harm your kid and that will help you feel better.

If necessary, leave the room in order to maintain self-control. Apologize to your kid and remind him that striking is never acceptable. Seek professional assistance if you can't control yourself.

Stay away from threats.

When you're enraged, your threats are always irrational. Your kids may not obey the rules again if threats are only effective if you are ready to follow through on them; this undermines your authority. Instead, explain to your youngster that you need some time to think about how to handle this lapse in discipline. It'll be worse than hearing a series of threats you won't follow through on.

Pay attention to your tone and word choice.

People who talk more calmly tend to be calmer, and those who speak more calmly tend to be calmer, according to research. Swearing or using other emotionally charged phrases exacerbates our feelings and the listeners, and the situation quickly spirals out of control. The way we talk and the words we use have the capacity to soothe or disturb ourselves and the person with whom we are conversing. Consider yourself a role model.

How long have you been enraged?

Don't be sucked in by your feelings of resentment. Put it away once you've listened to it and made the necessary adjustments. Keep in mind that rage is always a form of self-defense. It protects us from being exposed.

If you want to get rid of your anger, you should examine the pain or fear that lies behind it. Some parents worry about their children throwing tantrums, while others are saddened by their daughter's disdain for her family because she's too preoccupied with her pals. Your anger will subside as soon as you acknowledge and experience those underlying feelings. As a result, you'll be more equipped to help your youngster tackle a challenge that appeared intractable.

Make a list of appropriate methods to deal with anger and publish it for others to see.

Talk to your children about appropriate methods to deal with their feelings of frustration. Is there ever a time when hitting someone is acceptable? Is it OK to toss things? Is it OK to shout at someone? Keep in mind that the rules that govern your kid also govern you, as the example you set.

You and your family may then create a list of appropriate methods to deal with your feelings of frustration and display it on the fridge where everyone in the family can see it. Keep an eye on your phone when you're about to lose your cool.

- Ask for what you want, but don't attack the other person.

- Put on some music and let your fury out via dancing.

- Clap your hands around your own body when you're ready to strike.

Decide which fights are worth fighting.

When you have an argument with your kid, you deplete your child's emotional bank account. What counts most is how your kid respects other people, not how he or she behaves. This little annoyance may make you want to scream, but it's not worth going into the red in your relationship bank account. Keep in mind that the closer you and your kid are, the more likely he is to obey your instructions.

Be aware of the fact that you are a part of the issue.

As long as you're willing to open yourself up to emotional development, your kid will always point you in the right direction. It's difficult to be a calm parent if you're not since anything will set you off on your worst behavior. Every time we engage with our children, we have the ability to either soothe or aggravate the situation. Regardless of how irritated you are with your child's behavior; you do not have to remain a powerless bystander.

First and foremost, take responsibility for your own emotional well-being. If you can keep your cool in the face of your child's rage, she may not become an angel overnight, but you'll be surprised at how much better she behaves.

Keep seeking for methods to discipline that promote improved conduct and keep searching for new ways to do so.

Disciplining with fury does more harm than good, as study demonstrates, since it creates a feedback loop that reinforces bad conduct.

For some parents, learning that children are seldom disciplined and that parental screaming is rare comes as a surprise. Parent-child connection and supporting children with their needs and upsets are the primary means of enforcing these limits and expectations for conduct. A growing body of evidence shows that children raised in emotionally aware homes are better equipped to regulate their conduct as adults.

Chapter 5:

Calming Techniques

How do you keep your kid from getting into fights all the time? As if that weren't enough, the ability to stay cool is what will get you through any crisis scenario. Keeping your calm when your youngster is agitated, nervous, or furious is half the fight. By dousing the flames with water rather than pouring additional fuel from your own emotional tank, you may put out the fire instead of extinguishing it yourself.

I know it's difficult to keep your cool while dealing with children, particularly if you have a youngster that yells and screams. Even though you know what you should be doing, that doesn't mean you can really accomplish it. How come? In the heat of battle, our emotional brain becomes over excited and we lose sight of our rational brain, even though we know what the appropriate thing to do is. 'Reactivity' develops when our brains are bombarded with emotions. Even the most difficult of children may cause you to lash out at them, scream and shut down, all of which are ineffective ways to cope with them.

When it comes to parenthood, we've all been there. When we connect with our children, we might experience a range of emotions, such as anger, perplexity, hurt, disappointment, and fury. In a matter of seconds, these sentiments may either excite or overwhelm us. We are all susceptible in various ways, and each of those 'triggers' forces us to confront our flaws, our shame, our worries, our phobias from our upbringing, and the parts of ourselves we'd rather hide.

Our children, just by being children, may cause us to feel a range of negative feelings. These feelings might drive us to make bad parenting judgments if we respond to them in the wrong way. We don't always have our children's best interests in mind while we're attempting to protect ourselves. When we're agitated, we're more likely to talk harshly and unkindly to them, and we're more likely to regret it afterwards. Gloom follows. To understand the difference between acceptable and unacceptable conduct is critical. As a result of our inability to accept our own feelings, we act them out with our children and our loved ones in destructive ways. We have a lot more difficult time helping our children develop and cope with life if our sentiments dominate us rather than us being able to regulate them. Maintaining a cool demeanor and resisting the need to react angrily when your kid presses your buttons is the most important thing you can do.

In order to be a calm parent, here are some tips.

Staying Calm

Consider things from a new angle. Anger towards your child can be reduced if you can alter your perspective. Every day, our children can irritate and frustrate us to the point of exhaustion. Then, keep in mind that most of the time, they're acting like kids. Angry feelings are natural, but they aren't directed at anybody else. Our patience, tolerance (or lack thereof), attitude, and outlook all play a role. The initial reaction when your child swears at you is to feel upset, dissatisfied, and to place the blame for his conduct. No matter what, he should be held accountable for his actions and face the consequences. Remember, though, that your youngster is only being a kid and doing this. Making sure he accepts responsibility and makes restitution is part of your role as his leader.

Teenagers are tasked with trying out new roles and relationships as they grow up. It's upsetting and upsetting for us, but it's normal for them to go through this stage of growth. Children learn about the principles of cause and effect when they break the rules and push themselves to their limits. It aids individuals in making sense of their own life. This is completely normal and expected. Instead of blaming children for their actions, our role is to teach them better conduct via the use of natural consequences.

I'm not saying we should accept terrible conduct, but I'm recommending that you try not to be angry at them for their developmentally-appropriate activities—even if those actions are unpleasant or upsetting to you. It's possible that your lack of patience is the root of your dissatisfaction, in which case it's up to you to work it out, not theirs.

It's crucial to find techniques to lessen our rage at our children. Taking responsibility for our own thoughts, feelings, and behaviors can help others do the same. Understanding and processing our own emotions is the responsibility of everyone. In order to teach our children how to accept responsibility for their actions, we must avoid blaming them for our own sentiments and reactions.

Make a list of what you're thinking and feeling. Think about what you're about to feel before you let out a big sigh of relief. Is it annoyance, angst, or pain that's got you down? Use your own name to identify it as belonging to you. Tell yourself, "I feel [blank] when I watch my child performing X, Y or Z." When I see my kid not helping out around the house, I get angry because I feel like a bad parent. Fearing that he would never accept responsibility and shame for not doing his job, I'm trying to find other work. Once you've done that, consider what you need to improve on personally and what feedback you should provide to your child. It's important to digest what's yours and then select what counsel to provide to your child as a responsible parent, in other words "I either need to think about how I can increase my efficacy as a parent or accept that I have done all that I can," you could tell yourself in this situation. "I have to cope with my own guilt and fear for my child's future."

After acknowledging our feelings, we may begin to soothe them, understand them, change them, and release them. We won't let our hurt sentiments seep out onto others. Adults must be capable of acknowledging and accepting their own sentiments, even when they are difficult to express. To be a good parent, we must first understand our own sentiments of dread, inadequacy, or shame—or whatever other sensations we've tried to avoid being provoked by our children. Observe how easy it is to place the blame on the person or thing that set them off. Keep in mind that our children just serve to arouse sentiments already present inside us; they do not create them. To put the blame on our children is to abdicate our duty of self-care.

Take a deep breath and some time to reflect. Your youngster can learn from your experience of managing challenging emotions. Take a few deep breaths, calm yourself down, and come up with a strategy for dealing with this circumstance. Talk to you later. It's a good indicator to take a few deep breaths and think about the best way to cope with a problem when you're feeling a little heated inside. Calming yourself down is also teaching your children how to calm themselves down. Because of this, the techniques of pause, inhalation, and contemplation are helpful. Adrenaline is released when you are under threat, whether physically or mentally. As a parent, you may feel intimidated when your child refuses to listen and you are unsure of what to do. Prepare for "fight or flight" by emptying your brain's energy for your muscles and putting it back into your body. To avoid saying anything you later regret, take a moment to pause, breathe, and consider before you speak. If you don't have them, you won't have access to the portion of your brain that can make excellent judgments, therefore you won't be able to address the challenges you face.

Focus on the positive and let go of the negative. Take a step back and realize that worrying over your child is a bad thing. Worrying also makes your youngster uneasy because he starts to feel that there is nothing within him to be worried about. He gets increasingly agitated. However, how can you not be concerned about a challenging child who is always making bad decisions? As a result, our minds are filled with visions of the worst-case scenarios. You should be aware, however, that the more you worry and dwell on your fears, the more a neural pathway is built in your brain, making anxiety simpler and easier. As a result, you're more concerned, not less. Try to focus on good outcomes rather than negative ones in your mind. After all, you have no idea what will happen. You'll feel less agitated if you imagine a better outcome. There's a higher possibility of directing your youngster properly if your brain performs better when you're less stressed. Inadvertently, a good thing can result from optimistic thought. Anger (or any response) can have an adverse effect on the quality of your relationships with others. Relationships can be damaged through long-term bad encounters.

A family's ability to remain calm is infectious. A tranquil family is the result of a calm individual. Additionally, you'll be teaching your children how to calm down in any scenario, which is a vital life skill for everyone to learn.

Breathing Methods of Calming Down

I've mentioned taking deep breaths. If we're venturing into the world of breathing to remain calm, there is a lifestyle dedicated to this discipline that's worth checking out.

Yoga!

I know, you didn't invest in a yoga book, but you are interested in keeping your calm when it comes to your children. As I've said earlier, there is no off switch that'll make you calm every time you're triggered. You're investing in a better lifestyle that'll lead to healthier relationships.

Yoga has long been revered for its therapeutic properties, which vary from its ability to stabilize metabolism to its capacity to increase range of motion and flexibility. Some people may be shocked to learn that yoga positions, breathing techniques, and mental exercises may all be used to help manage stress and anger, as well as other negative emotions.

Honestly, most of us can acknowledge that at some point in our lives, we've been so enraged that our moods were sour for the rest of the day, or our interactions with other people were thrown off. Despite the fact that anger is as vital as happiness in our lives, there are moments when we require techniques for calming down and refocusing our attention on the task at hand. Traditional and non-traditional practices that are linked to many of yoga's teachings can be used to calm anger when it first arises.

First and foremost, you must come to terms with the reality that you are upset. The first line of defense against an angry outburst or outbursts is to take a few deep, cleansing breaths. Yoga and meditation emphasize self-actualization, so once you've acknowledged that you feel angry, it's vital to evaluate what may happen if you lose control of your anger. Several breathing techniques and yoga positions may be helpful if you've tried these suggestions and your tension or anger is still out of control.

The following are five yoga asanas and recommendations from the mat that can help you manage your anger:

As one of the most calming poses, **Savasana** (Corpse Pose) is highly regarded for its ability to soothe the body and mind. Lay on your back with your arms relaxed at your sides and your palms facing up to achieve Savasana. Allow your feet to relax and your breathing to return to a regular pace. It's important to let your mind wander until you've reached a state of full relaxation.

The Child's Pose is a terrific way to remain in touch with our feelings and to build the mind-body connection. Child's Pose is a restorative pose that targets the muscles and the mind at the same time. To begin the Child's Pose, go down on your knees. Pull yourself up and lay your head on the ground with your arms at your sides. Reach your arms out in front of you in an extended Child's Pose to loosen up your shoulders and open your chest.

The Three Part's Breath is an effective way to deal with anger through the practice of nose breathing, which is a long-standing tradition in yoga. The Three-Part Breath is an excellent way to improve your ability to breathe through your nose. Simple and fulfilling, the Three-Part Breath is one of the simplest and most satisfying yogic breathing techniques. Slow and steady washing may bring about a sense of calm and harmony. It is both cleansing and revitalizing at the same time. To practice the Three-Part Breath, stand straight and inhale, bringing your breath all the way down into your abdomen, then up through your rib cage, and out through your neck and chest. Release any tension in your body by taking a deep breath out. To get the most out of this exercise, make sure your inhalation and exhalation times are exactly the same.

Relaxation is the fourth step. Calming and centering oneself may be achieved by the slow and deliberate inhalation and exhalation of breath. Additionally, it is a simple workout that may be used to combat stress and anger in daily life by reducing blood pressure and slowing the pulse rate (Shaw, 2013). Relaxation Breath may be practiced by lying comfortably on your back and letting go of any stress in your body. Your right hand should be placed on your chest and your left hand should be placed on the upper section of your abdomen. Only raise and lower your left hand as you inhale and exhale when you're breathing. As long as you don't move your right hand, you're good to go. Inhalation and exhalation should be given equal time.

Breathing exercises may not work for you if you can't sit still with your anger, so try something more severe! A sequence of positions can help you swiftly expel anger while also providing the hormone boost that comes with doing out. Half Sun Salutation to Plank Pose to Savasana or Child's Pose is a fantastic three-part series of exercises. With your feet together and your hands folded in front of you, begin with the Half Sun Salutation (as if you were praying). Sweep your arms up and focus on your fingers as you inhale, being careful to maintain your lower back pulled out. Exhale deeply, keeping your head tucked down as you fold forward with your palms on the floor. After that, take a deep breath in while folding forward from the hips, and then raise your arms back over your head so that your palms touch. You may hold this position for as long as necessary. Plank Pose is a perfect follow-up to the Half Sun Salutation. Holding a push-up stance is all that is required to attain Plank Pose. Hold this stance for as long as you can, starting with your hands parallel and shoulder-width apart, making sure your legs are straight. The final stance you'll want to try is Child's Pose, which is a restorative pose.

Chapter 6:

How To Control Your

Emotions

Is it possible to control your emotions?

The emotions that come up for you are beyond your control, but your actions are within your grasp. The mere fact that you are enraged with someone does not imply that you will express your feelings to that person. A person who claims to be unable to regulate their emotions is generally more concerned with the fact that they believe to be unable to regulate their actions. It becomes OK to be furious when you understand that you are not required to hit someone every time you feel that way. It is possible to just experience and digest an emotion without acting on it.

It is only when you see your emotions as signs to what is happening in your life, and you do not criticize yourself for experiencing whatever it is that you are able to make a decision about how to behave or respond. The emotional and cognitive aspects of your mind work together to assist you in solving problems and arriving at the most appropriate solution for you.

As a result, the quick answer is that you cannot 'control' your feelings. Nevertheless, if you follow the tactics for accepting your emotions as they arise, you will discover that you no longer need to let your emotions govern you.

Both you and your child are experiencing feelings. If you want to assist them in developing their emotional maturity, you must ensure that they are not exposed to you losing your anger with them or others in your immediate vicinity.

Managing Your Emotions

- **Pay attention to your emotions.**

Feelings are neither correct nor incorrect. It is what you do with your sentiments that determines whether they are beneficial or harmful. Whatever you do, it's critical that you pay attention to and accept your emotions so that you can make a deliberate decision about how to behave rather than reacting in a reactive manner.

- **Examine your child's conduct in the context of his or her developmental stage and temperament.**

Because the meaning you ascribe to your kid's conduct has an influence on how you manage your own emotions and reactions to the behavior in question, it is vital that you set realistic expectations for your child. It is more likely that you will react in a way that escalates the situation rather than one that calms your kid if you see the action as manipulative or as being intended to be painful (for example, biting or punching). Furthermore, powerful, furious emotions almost seldom result in the teaching of effective coping techniques. You may approach your kid with empathy if, on the other hand, you perceive these actions in the framework of normal growth. This will increase the likelihood that you will respond calmly and effectively to your child.

- Remember that you cannot force your child to do anything, including eating, sleeping, peeing, pooping, talking, or stopping a tantrum.

Your response to your children's activities is something you have complete control over, as it is this response that directs and molds their conduct. If having a tantrum results in more TV time, a later bedtime, or just more of your attention (a key desire for older siblings coping with serious rivalry), your toddler is putting two and two together and making an important assessment: "Tantrums are effective!" This is a fantastic technique! You can put that one in the winner's circle."

Putting Everything Together

Let's look at an example scenario:

When his mother, Lauren, tells him that the playdate has ended and it is time for Liam to go home, three-year-old Jonah declares, "You are the meanest mother, and I despise you," he kicks her in the shins.

Step 1: Pay attention to your emotions:

When Lauren becomes angry, she wants to scream, "You are the most unappreciative child I have ever met!" It has been 2 hours since Liam arrived, and I have put aside everything I needed to accomplish in order to oversee, bake cookies with you, set up the painting project, and so on and so forth. "There's never enough of anything!" But she understands that retaliating violently will not teach her child anything and will just add to the two of them suffering. She takes a few long breaths and considers how she would reply in order to assist Jonah in learning to control his powerful emotions and accept the boundary.

- **Listen to and affirm your child's feelings.**

It is at this point that having realistic expectations is important. Lauren reminds herself that even at the age of three, children are still primarily motivated by their emotions, and that the objective is to assist Jonah in learning to cope with the frustrations and disappointments of life as best she can. As a result, she informs him quietly, "I understand that you are upset and outraged that Liam has to return home. You're having a great time playing with him. When a playdate comes to an end, it is always difficult. However, you will be OK." It is critical to indicate that you have faith in your child's ability to cope with his or her unpleasant emotional experiences. When you swoop in to make everything great, you unintentionally give the message that he is incapable of dealing with disappointment, making it less likely that he will master this vital skill in the future.

- **Lastly, if your youngster tosses out some bait, don't fall for it.**

When it comes to obtaining something they desire, such as more television time or additional dessert, or avoiding doing something they dislike, such as getting dressed in the morning or brushing their teeth, young children will employ every method at their disposal. Ignoring habits that you believe will not benefit your child in the actual world is the most effective method of eliminating them. For Lauren to not answer Jonah's provocation, "You are the meanest mommy…" suggests that she is not responding to the provocation. When she throws out bait, she makes sure that it does not detract attention from the boundary she is placing, which is generally the aim of doing so: controlling other people's activities and keeping the child out of something he or she is uncomfortable with.

The fourth step is to define the boundaries and suggest alternatives: "It's alright to be sad and furious, but it's not appropriate to kick. Kicking is painful. I'm sure you don't mean to injure me; you're simply having a hard time keeping your body under control because you're feeling so unhappy. Consequently, you have an option between taking a break to relax your mind and body or helping to prepare supper by chopping carrots and putting them in the salad." If Jonah is unable to pull himself together at this time, Lauren will simply move on, demonstrating to him by her actions that she is willing to accept his being sad and disappointed and that she has faith in his capacity to calm himself. This leaves Jonah with the option of continuing to be sad or pulling himself together and spending time with his mother.

The ability to manage one's own emotions allows one to feel more in control and allows one to respond calmly and effectively to even the most demanding of actions.

Chapter 7:

Show and Teach Empathy

Every waking moment of the day, young children are paying close attention to the environment around them. They pay close attention to how their parents and caregivers speak, eat, respond to circumstances, and interact with people, among other things. You are the very first instructor your child ever had! Infants and toddlers are remarkable little pupils, recalling everything their parents and caregivers do and say even days and weeks after the fact. Your interactions with your children, as well as their relationships with their family members, friends, babysitters, and even the things that they see on television, teach them far more than you may be aware of. MSU Extension reminds parents that it is critical to carefully consider what they say and do in front of their children, and to be mindful of what they are seeing on television and in other media to ensure that what they are learning is what you want them to be learning!

The average amount of time that young children spend watching television each day is three hours, according to research findings (Lerner, 2016). In order to keep children entertained, caregivers frequently turn to television and movies, and many families say that the television is left on throughout the day, even when the family goes on to other activities such as sleep and mealtimes. Do you believe that your children are gaining knowledge through their television watching? According to the research, they are! To the contrary, with only 20 seconds of television viewing, toddlers as young as 14 months are able to imitate activities they see on the screen. How much do you believe a small toddler might learn from one hour of television viewing?

Keep in mind that your children are paying attention and mimicking everything you do. Make intelligent decisions about your words and actions. You must use extreme caution in everything you do and say. Begin to set a healthy example for your children as early as possible, even when they are infants and toddlers.

Consider your house as your child's initial educational environment. What do you want people to take away from this experience? Right from the outset, young toddlers are learning from their 'teachers' or other adults in their environment.

Every individual your child comes into contact with is imparting knowledge to them. Take advantage of their incredible learning skills! Infants have a strong desire to imitate facial expressions. In fact, kids as little as a few hours old may imitate an adult who puts their tongue out by sticking their tongue out themselves. If you grin at them, they will try to reciprocate with a smile. As newborns grow older, they become increasingly more adept at imitating your movements. Holding the phone in the same manner as you do, combing your hair, mirroring your motions, and speaking in the same tone of voice as you.

Why is this so important?

We all need to learn this because if you act on your triggers and display enough anger to your children, they will not forget what you've done. Their actions will be influenced in part by the level of rage you displayed.

Empathy is something you must model for your children.

Being Empathetic

Empathy is the ability to understand how another person is experiencing in a given circumstance and to respond with consideration and consideration. This is a difficult technique to master since it requires a great deal of concentration. Being empathetic includes:

1. Being able to empathize with another person means that a child.

2. Understanding that he is a separate individual, his own person.

3. Understanding that others can have different thoughts and feelings than he does.

4. Recognizing the common feelings that most people experience—happiness, surprise, anger, disappointment, sadness, and so on.

It is possible for him to look at a specific event (like as seeing a peer say good-bye to a parent at childcare) and picture how he, and therefore his buddy, could feel at that moment; and

In that particular scenario, may anticipate what kind of answer might be suitable or comforting—for example, providing his pal a favorite toy or teddy bear to console her.

Empathy has reached a number of important milestones.

Understanding and demonstrating empathy are the consequence of a variety of social-emotional abilities that emerge during a child's early years of development. The following are some very significant anniversaries:

1. Building a solid, robust, and loving relationship with you is one of the first major goals to achieve. Your child's ability to be accepted and understood by you will aid him in his future ability to accept and understand others.

2. Babies begin to make social references when they are around 6 months old. In this circumstance, a baby will turn to his or her parent or another loved one to measure his or her reaction to a person or a certain event

Example: When her father welcomes a new guest to their house, a 7-month-old baby looks at her father attentively to determine whether or not this new person is good and safe. The baby's reaction to the guest is influenced by the parent's reaction to the visitor. (This is why parents are urged to be happy and comforting while saying goodbye to their children at childcare, rather than frantically hovering about them.) It conveys the notion that "you are in a nice spot" and that "all will be OK." Social reference or being attentive to a parent's behavior in unfamiliar situations, aids in the understanding of the environment and the people in it by the newborns themselves.

3. Toddlers will begin to acquire a theory of mind between the ages of 18 and 24 months old (Lerner, 2016). The moment a child discovers that, just as he has his own thoughts, feelings, and aspirations, others have their own thoughts and ideas, which may be diametrically opposed to their own.

4. Toddlers will begin to recognize themselves in a mirror when they are between the ages of 18 and 24 months (Lerner, 2016). This indicates that a youngster has a clear grasp of his or her own identity as a distinct individual.

You can help your toddler develop empathy by following these suggestions.

- Understand and empathize with your child. "Do you have a fear of that dog?" would be an appropriate question. He is a friendly dog; however he is barking very loudly. That may be a frightening prospect. "I'll hold you till he comes around the corner."

- Discuss the emotions of other people. Take the following example: "Kayla is upset because you removed her toy car. If you could please return Kayla's vehicle and then pick another one to play with."

- Make suggestions on how youngsters might demonstrate empathy. To give an example, "Let's go get Jason some ice for his sprain."

- Be a role model for others. When you develop strong, respectful connections with people and engage with them in a kind and loving manner, your kid will take note and emulate your behavior.

- Make use of 'I' messages. It is important to be self-aware in communicating, as demonstrated by the following example: "I don't like it when you strike me." It's a physical pain.

- Recognize and validate your child's challenging feelings. When our child is unhappy, angry, or disappointed, we often rush to try to remedy the situation as soon as possible in order to make the feelings go away because we want to protect him from any further suffering. These emotions, on the other hand, are a natural part of life, and children must learn to manage with them. It has been shown that identifying and affirming uncomfortable sentiments can actually assist children in learning to cope with them: You're enraged because I turned the television off for you. I get what you're saying. You enjoy spending time with your animals on your animal show. It's quite okay to be enraged. As soon as you are finished being upset, you may either help me prepare a delicious meal or play in the kitchen while mommy makes our sandwiches for lunch. Using this sort of approach also helps youngsters develop the ability to empathize with those who are going through tough times.

- Make use of role-playing games. As you play, talk with older toddlers about their feelings and their empathy. For example, you might have your child's plush hippo express displeasure at his stuffed pony's insistence on taking turns with him. Then inquire of your youngster as to how he or she believes the pony feels. What should we say to this obnoxious hippo?

- Consider the appropriateness of the phrase "I'm sorry." We frequently need our toddlers to say, "I'm sorry" as a means of encouraging them to accept responsibility for their behavior. However, many toddlers are unable to comprehend the entire meaning of these phrases. While it may feel 'right' for them to say "I'm sorry," saying this phrase does not necessarily aid in the development of empathy in toddlers. A more significant method is to assist youngsters in concentrating on the sentiments of the other person: Look at Sierra, Chandra; she's in a bad mood. She's weeping out loud. She's touching the area on her arm where you smacked her. Let's see whether she's all right. As a result, youngsters may form a link between the action (shoving) and the reaction (shoving back) (a friend who is sad and crying).

- Please be patient. Empathy is something that takes time to develop. Your child is unlikely to be a fully empathic human by the time he or she reaches the age of three. Although some teens and even adults have not totally mastered this talent, this is not the case for everyone! In reality, a large and quite typical part of being a toddler is concentrating on oneself, one's own, and one's own. Remember that empathy is a difficult talent to master and will continue to grow throughout your child's lifetime.

Ideas for Practicing Empathy

Make contact with new people.

According to the findings of academics, attempting to picture how someone else feels is frequently insufficient. Fortunately, the remedy is straightforward: simply ask them. Curiosity, according to Jodi Halpern, a psychiatrist and bioethics professor at the University of California, Berkeley, who studies empathy, lies at the heart of empathy. "It's about understanding what another person's life is like in its particulars."

It's worth a shot.

Attempt to strike up a discussion with someone you don't know well or ask a coworker or neighbor you don't know well to lunch. Take it a step further and inquire as to how they are doing and what their daily routine is like.

Follow individuals on social media who come from a variety of diverse backgrounds than your own (different race, religion, or political persuasion).

If possible, put your phone and other displays away when you're having discussions, even with individuals that you see on a daily basis, so that you can pay attention to their facial expressions and other body language.

Try living someone else's life for a while.

According to Helen Riess, a psychiatrist at Harvard Medical School and the chief scientist of Empathetics, which provides empathy training for health-care professionals, "don't simply put yourself in someone else's shoes; walk a mile in their shoes."

Attend another church, mosque, synagogue, or other institution of worship for a few weeks while someone else attends yours, or travel to a hamlet in a poor country and donate your time and talents. Travel to a new neighborhood or strike up a chat with a homeless person in your own area to broaden your perspective.

If someone's behavior is upsetting you, consider why it is so. To begin with, acknowledge the fact that your adolescent may be worried, but go on to say: "I understand you're stressed." Consider what it's like for him to go about his daily routine-how long his bus commute is, how much schoolwork he has, and how much sleep he gets, for example.

Joining forces to advance a common cause

When people work together on a project, they are able to build on each other's individual expertise and humanity, while also minimizing the differences that can divide them. Rachel Godsil, a law professor at Rutgers University and co-founder of the Perception

Institute, which studies how humans form biases and provides workshops on how to overcome them, said this was a good thing.

- Work on a communal garden is underway.

- Participate in political organizing.

- Participate on a religious committee.

If you have suffered sorrow or loss, you may share your feelings with others who have gone through something similar to you.

According to Dr. Halpern, "my magic elixir would be for communities to have meaningful, emotional initiatives that speak to their pain and vulnerabilities."

For example, she discovered in her research that when women from the former Yugoslavia came together across ethnic groups to assist in the search for the bodies of family members who had gone missing, they came to care for and respect one another despite the conflicts that existed between their ethnic groups. In a similar vein, Israeli and Palestinian families who have lost a member of their direct family as a result of the violence in the region have formed an organization known as Parents Circle - Families Forum.

Be up front and honest with yourself.

According to Erin L. Thomas, a partner at Paradigm, which assists businesses with diversity and inclusion strategies, "Bias is an inherent component of the human experience." When we use mental shortcuts and draw assumptions about the individuals in our immediate environment, this is considered adaptive. What matters is that we are actively engaged in combating it.

Again, conversing with others is beneficial.

According to Ms. Thomas, one of the most effective methods to face bias and privilege in your life is to learn about other people's everyday lives and evaluate how they are different from yours.

She explained that it might be as easy as having lunch with a coworker and learning about their daily routines. Perhaps you'll discover that they leave early to care for a family member or that they take an alternative route to work because they are terrified of contact with law enforcement. Perhaps they don't feel heard in meetings, or they have difficulty finding a convenient time and location to pump breast milk during the day.

"The more you hear about the things that other people have to factor into their day, the more you notice the things that you don't have to pay attention to," Ms. Thomas explained. "The more you hear about the things that other people have to factor into their day, the more you recognize the things that you don't have to pay attention to."

Take action NOW!

Putting your privileges to work on behalf of people that do not have access is the next step after you have acknowledged your rights.

Here are a few examples on how to go about it:

Make a monetary donation to organizations that assist those in need or attend a rally in their support.

Speak out if someone makes a prejudiced remark or interrupts you while you are working. According to Ms. Thomas, this is especially vital to do when you are not a member of the group that is being undermined.

The following may be said if someone interrupted: "I believe she was still in the process of expressing her thought; let's give her a chance to complete before we go on."

To respond to someone who makes an inappropriate joke or insulting remark, just state: "You have just said something that is disrespectful."

Boost the volume of other people's voices.

It is sometimes the most effective thing you can do to provide a place for others outside your group to speak that will have the most impact.

Here are a few examples on how to go about it:

You should look for articles published by members of underrepresented groups or members of the community that the article is about if you wish to share them online.

In the event that you hear someone dismiss or claim credit for someone else's idea, you may say something like: "She has a valid point; let's debate it more."

It's not about you at all.

You should keep in mind that you don't have to know everything about someone in order to make them feel valued.

You may advocate for things that will benefit others, even if they do not directly touch you, such as campaigning for paid maternity leave even if you are not a parent or assisting in the organization of an event for LGBTQ coworkers even if you are not a member of the LGBTQ community.

It is not appropriate to draw generalizations about individuals based on your personal experiences. Consider the following scenarios while interviewing coworkers about their lives: don't assume they have an opposite-sex partner, three healthy children, or a lovely, large house when you question them about their lives.

The researchers define office housekeeping as an unglamorous task such as bringing coffee for a meeting or planning a colleague's farewell party. In the workplace, women and people of color perform more of this type of labor. Recognize when this occurs, and if you are not already a member of one of these groups, volunteer to take on these responsibilities and recruit others to do so as well.

Teach Empathy to Children

Since they are newborns, children have demonstrated empathy by mimicking facial expressions and learning to smile back at those who have hurt them. For example, everyone who has witnessed toddlers squabbling over toys knows that it takes longer for them to learn to consider other people's points of view. Parents and caregivers may, however, influence their children's empathy in a variety of ways.

Based on the facial expressions of characters in books or during creative play, ask children what they believe the characters are experiencing. You may also ask them what is happening to them in the tale.

Do not urge your child to express regret. Although it is a natural impulse, experts warn that it might backfire because it does not force them to really consider the other person's sentiments. Instead, ask queries such as, "How do you suppose he's feeling right now?" "Can you think of anything you could do to make him feel better?"

Assist your children in identifying and naming their emotions. Allow children to express their feelings when they are screaming out in frustration or rage, or when they don't want night to come or school to begin. You should also express your sentiments in front of them, utilizing the entire spectrum of emotional terminology available to you.

When you're talking to someone about an issue they're experiencing, such as with a sibling or a friend at school, encourage them to consider the other person's point of view.

Offer soup to a friend who is going through a difficult time, volunteer as a family in your community, or bring a welcome bouquet to a new family at school to demonstrate empathy and compassion.

Read aloud to them.

Like novels do for adults, children's books transport them into the lives and hearts of the characters they read about. The first step is to select books that include a broad cast of characters – such as powerful female leads, melanated children, and those with disabilities – so that children may see characters they relate with as well as those with which they do not identify.

Parents and caregivers may also use books to explore topics such as prejudice with their children. Members of the Little Feminist book club get novels, as well as activities and discussion questions, to use in discussing gender equality and diversity with both girls and boys.

Joining the book club is free. EmbraceRace has compiled a list of 26 children's books that may be used to initiate discussions on race.

According to Maria Russo, the children's books editor of *The New York Times Book Review,* these three titles are worth checking out:

Ezra Jack Keats' poem *The Snowy Day* is about a snowy day. Despite its age, the first full-color picture book focusing on an African-American youngster remains a moving work of art.

Pancho Rabbit and the Coyote is a children's book written by Duncan Tonatiuh. When a rabbit family attempts to travel north, they meet a number of difficulties.

In Cynthia Kadohata's short story *The Thing About Luck,* she writes: During the summer, a 12-year-old Japanese-American girl goes from the West Coast to the Midwest to live with her elderly grandparents.

And here are three novels that have been recommended by the members of the Little Feminist book club:

In *Drum Dream Girl,* written and drawn by Margarita Engle and Rafael López, the following is depicted: Based on a real tale, a young Cuban girl has a passion of becoming a drummer but is informed she would be unable to pursue her ambition because she is a girl.

As shown in *Jabari Jumps*, written by Gaia Cornwall, Jabari tackles his worries and exposes his vulnerability with the support of his father when attempting to leap from the diving board.

Introducing Teddy, written and drawn by Jessica Walton and Dougal MacPherson, is as follows: Unknown to the bear, the young human buddy learns from the bear that the bear is actually a female on the inside, and the friend embraces the bear for who it is.

Bias should be discussed.

Many parents, particularly white parents, strive to avoid discussing race, gender identity, financial level, or other disparities among individuals, believing that if they expose their children to a diverse range of experiences without making a big issue about it, their children will grow up free of prejudice.

However, research has demonstrated that this is not the case. Even preschoolers notice differences — and retain prejudices as a result. The fact that adults don't talk to their children about it might exacerbate the situation, as youngsters may end up adopting society preconceptions or believing that it is a taboo subject.

According to Dawn Dow, a sociologist at the University of Maryland who specializes on race and family, these talks generally begin much earlier in the day for families of color due to the necessity of doing so. Parents make every effort to safeguard their children from racism and to ensure that they are exposed to individuals who are similar to them.

Researchers advise having difficult conversations. Bring up sensitive issues such as race. Speak to children about racism, how boys and girls have not always been permitted to do the same things, how various families have varying degrees of financial resources, how people's bodies are all different shapes and sizes, and how families are made up of a variety of different people combinations.

It is important not to quiet children when they make comments about skin color or to skip over the portions of novels where characters are subjected to discrimination — these are the teaching moments. As an alternative, discuss prejudice and the reasons why it is wrong. "Yes, humans come in a variety of skin tones, just as you and I have a variety of hair hues," say the experts if they make a public statement.

Increase the diversity of their media intake, not only with stories of historical luminaries, but also with stories of children of color "doing regular things, enjoying their lives," according to Ms. Dow, who spoke at the event. She used the Nick Jr. program *Dora the Explorer* and the book *Lola at the Library* as examples of what she was talking about.

Parents are concerned that discussing race and racism with their children would lead to their children being racist, according to Jessica Calarco, a sociologist at Indiana University (Miller, 2020). However, the research indicates that this is not the case. It has been shown that children who have open and honest dialogues with their parents are more likely to understand and address structural injustices in our society.

Instruct them on how to combat stereotypes.

According to research, children are aware of stereotypes by the age of three (Miller, 2020). Encourage youngsters to participate in a wide range of activities and to spend time with a diverse group of friends to counteract these negative influences. In your own life, set an example by sharing household duties, beginning with your children.

It is important to tell youngsters that they are incorrect when they say things like "Boys don't play with dolls" or "Girls aren't strong at science." Identify and debate any prejudices that you observe in their television shows or books: "Is it extremely necessary for only boys to play baseball?" alternatively, "Why do you suppose it is the mother who does all of the cooking for the children?"

Teach children what to do if they are discriminated against or witness someone else being discriminated against and engage in role-playing with them. Educate them on how to say, 'Stop' or "That's mean," or how to stand next to the person who is being targeted, or how to seek the assistance of a trusted adult in an emergency.

Chapter 8:

Lead by Example

While parents aren't expected to be 'perfect,' raising happy, well-adjusted children isn't really that difficult in the majority of circumstances.

Children require affection. Children require clear limits. Children want a role model that they can look up to and learn from.

As a parent, your primary responsibility is to set a good example by modeling the sort of conduct that you want your children to exhibit themselves.

Of course, becoming a role model frequently entails taking a careful, honest look at one's own life and how one conducts oneself.

This type of self-examination might be difficult at times, but it is very important for your child's health and well-being in the long run.

You're the Mirror

As a parent, there are a variety of methods to lead by example, assisting your children in developing character and self-respect while also demonstrating: This is what it looks like when you're wonderful.

1. Do your absolute best. When it comes to your children, setting a good example is essential. All of the things you say and do are noticed by your children, and they copy your words and actions. Keep in mind how readily they might be swayed by outside forces. Make an effort to be your best.

2. Make sure you look after yourself. Being your best begins with taking excellent care of yourself, which includes getting adequate sleep, scheduling time for exercise, eating nutritious foods, and developing appropriate coping mechanisms to deal with bad emotions without exploding.

Exhausting yourself by always putting the needs of others before your own is not a wise decision. That is not the sort of future you want for your child, so don't set a bad example for him or her.

3. Demonstrate dependability. You don't want to raise a child who is unreliable and who disappoints others, so make a point of modeling dependability yourself.

That includes putting your child's needs first ("I told you that we'd go to the park after you cleaned up your room, so let's go!") rather than putting work or other obligations first all of the time. It also entails going above and above for your friends, family, coworkers, and everyone else in your life.

4. Take stock of your situation. Incorporating the habit of "checking in" to examine your own conduct is a lovely thing to do—and it's beneficial for your child to watch and hear you do it as well.

By stating something like: "Lately, I've been thinking that I might be spending too much time in front of the television, you can start a dialogue with your youngster."

"I'm feeling a little drained right now. I believe that I need to start eating healthy stuff again."

"Today I was filled with rage! I believe it is past time for me to examine my approach to dealing with disagreements with people."

Invite your child to participate in the discussion and share some of the topics that he or she would like to learn more about or better.

The concept that becoming a great person is a continuous effort is reinforced as a result of your actions in this way. There's always something new to learn and develop!

5. Maintain your integrity. Today's technology allows you to quickly and easily banish someone from your life by just pressing a button on a smartphone. Prove to your youngster what genuine devotion looks like by turning up to assist a buddy in need or by sticking with a local company owner who has serviced your family for years rather than jumping over to the newest low-cost mega-store.

6. Pay close attention. As children grow older, they tend to want greater freedom ("Mom, please don't come into my room!"), which is very understandable. However, as a parent, it is not your responsibility to be a "cool buddy." It is your responsibility to be a parent. This requires staying alert and making certain that your child is not in danger—even if your youngster considers you to be 'annoying.'

You may say anything along the lines of:

"You are extremely valuable to me, and it is my obligation to ensure that you are always healthy and safe. I hope that one day you will realize why it is my obligation to be so attentive and to take such good care of the individuals I care about most. Hopefully, if you ever have children, you'll be interested and sensitive to their needs as well."

7. Instill a healthy dose of skepticism in your young students (Gelb, 2019). Children are inherently trustworthy, and they actively seek out role models in their immediate environment to emulate. Instruct children on the fact that not all "role models" are trustworthy. In order to demonstrate healthy skepticism and the ability to "follow your instincts," you must first demonstrate healthy skepticism.

For example, when visiting a vehicle showroom, you may quietly turn to your child and tell him or her:

"These sellers are claiming that this is the finest offer in town, but I have a sneaking suspicion that they could be mistaken. Let's have a look at some additional automobile dealerships. It's critical to follow your instincts."

Accept responsibility when you have acted wrongly. In situations where you react badly, such as shouting furiously at your spouse because you're hungry and tired, don't justify your actions. Accept responsibility for your actions and acknowledge that you did anything wrong.

The ability to observe adults accepting responsibility for their actions—as well as enacting 'consequences' to remedy bad behavior—is beneficial for your child's development.

"When I shouted at your father, it escalated into a major argument, and I was unable to go for my run today. As a substitute, we're going to stay at home and spend some quality time together discussing. We're going to come up with a strategy to ensure that this doesn't happen again."

9. In the event that your kid behaves poorly, implement penalties. Despite the fact that many parents are hesitant to impose repercussions when their children disobey a rule, consistency is essential.

When your child engages in improper behavior, it is critical that you impose an appropriate punishment. This relates to lesson number three, which is to be trustworthy. Consistency and dependability are important to children's development. They are more likely to feel aimless and unsupported if they do not have it, and they are more likely to develop into adults who do not understand the need for consistency.

10. Get started right away. Generally, the behaviors that children adopt at a young age are carried over into their adult lives. In light of the fact that bad habits are difficult to break, one of the most important things you can do for your children is to set an example of conduct that positively forms their character and values and prepares them to lead responsible and productive lives from an early age.

The sooner you can get started, the better. The greater the degree of consistency, the better.

After everything is said and done, no matter what age your children are, it is never too late to begin modeling the behavior you want them to emulate—raising wonderful children who grow up to be awesome adults!

Chapter 9:

Make Your Child Feel Safe

We all want our children to be confident in their own skin, but what can parents and caregivers do to help their children feel better about themselves? As it turns out, one of the most important things caregivers can do for their children is to provide them with the opportunity to form a solid relationship with them. The term 'attachment' refers to the bond that exists between a kid and their primary caregiver. While a kid's attachment is good (or secure), this link can help the youngster feel comfortable even when the child is away from the caregiver and exploring the world. The wonderful thing about attachment is that a kid may truly absorb the emotions of safety and security that their parents provide them, allowing them to carry those sentiments with them wherever they go as they grow older. They have created an "inner functioning model" of their parents in this way. This means that we practically carry our loved ones with us in our bodies, brains, and emotions, even while we are separated from one another physically.

What is the relationship between "secure connection" and self-confidence?

The term "secure attachment" refers to a child's feeling of confidence in their caregiver, who they believe will react to their needs and keep them safe. As a person grows older, having a solid connection can lead to enhanced self-confidence, resilience, and high self-esteem.

Having a stable bond as a youngster allows them to create what is known in the field as a "safe foundation," from which they may have the confidence to venture out into the world and explore it (through crawling, walking, exploring objects, etc.). The safe basis that the kid has established as they grow older is what allows them to feel confident enough to explore the world away from their parents and to form relationships with classmates and others.

When it comes to promoting healthy attachment, is there a 'better' parenting method to employ?

There are numerous different parenting theories and culturally unique parenting methods, all of which promote healthy attachment in children. However, despite the fact that there are many positive aspects to the parenting style known as "Attachment Parenting," research has shown that it is no more effective at building secure attachment than other conventional parenting techniques (Slumberkins, 2020). The fact that there is no single best way to parent that will result in healthy parent-child attachment is something we want parents to understand. There are numerous approaches that are effective, and it is vital to pick the one that feels right to you.

Despite the fact that we want to do everything we can to suit our infant's requirements, it's crucial for parents to understand that they don't have to do everything flawlessly! Many parents these days are quite afraid that if they do not respond to their infant's wants immediately and completely accurately, they will lead their kid to develop an unhealthy attachment— fortunately, this is not the case! Knowing that we must satisfy our children's needs perfectly puts entirely too much pressure on ourselves, and it turns out that this isn't even beneficial in the end. In order for an infant to form a stable bond with its caregiver, the caregiver just has to be attentive to the baby approximately 30 percent of the time, according to research. Instead of reacting to the kid 'exactly,' what is crucial is that the youngster establishes a bond of trust with the parent, knowing that the parent will always be there for them and will make every effort to satisfy their needs. Also, if a parent makes a mistake (for example, attempts to put the kid down for a nap when the youngster is actually hungry), the parent may simply try again until the mistake is corrected. To put it another way, just show up and give your best... you don't have to be flawless!

What if my child experiences periods of insecurity?

Every individual, even those who have a stable bond, may experience feelings of insecurity, or worry from time to time—especially when embarking on a new endeavor. Young children, in particular, might be particularly susceptible to emotions of anxiety associated with being separated from their parents. The sense of being self-conscious in social situations, as well as sadness when a parent sets you off at school, is a natural aspect of growth and does not necessarily imply the presence of attachment discomfort. Children adore their parents to such an extent that it might be difficult to separate them. Parents can try their best to enable their children to experience all of the emotions that they are experiencing without feeling the need to modify them. You can say something like, "It's understandable that you're nervous; we're all nervous when we meet new people. Let's attempt to say hello to each other."

Can you tell me what I can do right now to make my child feel more safe and secure?

When it comes to infants, try your best to suit their requirements, but remember to take care of yourself as well! It might be difficult to strike a balance in the early months but prioritizing your own needs can put you in a better position to fulfill the needs of your kid. Building a stable relationship with your child does not require you to be with him or her all of the time. It is acceptable to take pauses and call for assistance; doing so will not have an adverse effect on your relationship with your kid.

With young children: It is critical to maintain a good mix of caring, nurturing, and fun, as well as structure, boundaries, and limitations, while dealing with children under the age of five. When children have access to both ends of this range, they are more comfortable and confident in their ability to explore the world. This is also an excellent period for allowing for and encouraging your child's emotional development. Make it clear to them that their emotions are OK when they have a meltdown (not necessarily their actions).

If you have a kid who is older and more autonomous, it's crucial to provide them the opportunity to explore in a secure and developmentally appropriate environment. Allowing children the freedom to explore gives the message to them that you have faith in them. Keep in mind, too, that even older children require the love and connection of their parents. Make it clear to your elder family members, via words and acts, that you are always linked, even while you are separated.

There is no one technique to make your kid feel safe and secure, but keeping the following points in mind is a fantastic place to begin:

- Establish and maintain a secure bond with your child.

- Allow your children to experience their emotions.

- Promoting constructive debates should be encouraged.

- Maintain a sense of fun while maintaining clear boundaries.

Your Child Feeling Unsafe

Emotional safety helps your kid to be honest and not lie, to own and accept responsibility for mistakes, and to be open and honest with others. Children require an environment in which they may feel emotionally secure, which means that they must be able to trust that their feelings and thoughts will be treated with the compassion and respect that they deserve in their family. This degree of trust enables youngsters to be completely honest about how they actually feel and what they truly require. It's also what permits them to be honest about their wrongdoings and what is required for your child to avoid resorting to lying as a defense mechanism when confronted with their mistakes. This degree of emotional safety enables children to recognize and communicate what they are uncomfortable with, which is a critical component in protecting children from many sorts of abuse, including sexual assault.

A kid who is frequently fearful of criticism and rejection from their parents may expend a great deal of energy in order to conceal their wrongdoings, which can result in lying, harboring secrets, and being excessively defensive and reactive in their behavior. If a kid's errors and upsets are treated with dismissiveness, harsh criticism, or shutting down (such as being ordered to calm down or sent to their room), rather than with caring and support, the child begins to internalize the belief that it is not acceptable for them to express their feelings. Even if they don't appear to be unhappy on the outside, something on the inside is frequently shutting down, and they might grow progressively uneasy. Parenting children can be difficult, especially when the child's behavior causes distress to another. However, there are a variety of communication and relationship skills that parents can learn that will assist them in maintaining the connection even when disciplining (teaching) their children, such as assertiveness and listening skills.

It is essential for children to know that their parents notice and trust in their goodness and potential despite all of their difficulties, and that the connection is more important than any learning edges or mistakes. Children are tremendously reliant on their parents' love, acceptance, and approval, which they get in plenty. A major source of incentive for a youngster to do the right thing is taken away when they do not have their parents' approval. While most children will strive hard to keep their parent's warmth and affection, the majority of children will resist the idea of having to earn it since the absence of unconditional warmth and love may be quite painful for them.

Previous research has shown that children are far more subject to stress in the home and disagreements with their parents (or between their parents) than previously thought to exist. The more extreme consequences of yelling at or beating children were formerly thought to have a detrimental influence on the child's confidence, social skills, and trust in their parents. This has changed recently. Although society is slowly but steadily acknowledging (based on a large body of research) that children require a sense of safety and security not just physically, but also emotionally, this recognition is gaining ground. Unfortunately, it is quite simple for a parent to make their child fearful of their wrath or judgment because of their own fear. A surprising number of parents believe it is necessary to inculcate fear into their children, completely oblivious to the reality that when a youngster feels secure and safe with their parents, cooperation is not only feasible, but far more probable and readily provided as well. Children who learn to dread their parents suffer enormously in terms of their sense of security and self-confidence, as well as in terms of their relationship with their parents. It is critical for a kid to feel emotionally comfortable in their home, and that they do not fear their own parents.

They become defensive and use a significant amount of energy deflecting criticism, as well as feeling generally disturbed and unsupported when they live with the worry of being spoken to harshly. It's common for youngsters who feel emotionally insecure to complain about a variety of things their parents do in an attempt to convey the underlying grievances that they can't quite understand or articulate correctly. Both the kid and the parent may be perplexed by this since the parent may believe they are doing everything for their child and that they are satisfying all of their child's (at least bodily) requirements, yet their child remains restless, cranky, and unappreciative. Whenever children feel shut off by their parents, it develops obstacles to open communication and affection in the parent-child connection that present themselves over time as aggressive behavior, pouting, disobedience, reluctance to listen or cooperate, and a variety of other issues.

Crying helps to maintain the heart in good shape. According to the research, if a child is discouraged from expressing their true feelings and from allowing themselves to cry or talk to release those pent up feelings, that child is more likely to act out those feelings through unhealthy behaviors such as aggression towards others, or they may shut down, becoming aloof, bored, sarcastic, or passive-aggressive in other ways (Simperingham, 2013). When parents realize how important it is to allow their children to express their (Simperingham, 2013) full range of emotions, they quickly realize how important it is for their children to remain open, honest, and vulnerable with their feelings, as well as the importance of a child seeking support and listening from their parents Simperingham, 2013). Children may restore their balance when they scream out in the midst of their parents' loving support.

Many parents say that their child has learned to cry less often than necessary, and, sadly, has also learned to conceal their sensitivity in the process (Simperingham, 2013). According to Aletha Solter, the youngster may have formed a control pattern. A control pattern is any approach that a parent routinely utilizes to distract a kid from their distress (for example, food or electronics), which the youngster learns to identify with their need when unhappy. It is conceivable that instead of sobbing out their displeasure, children would need comfort food or access to a screen. The most common control behaviors are food, drink, entertainment, and cuddly objects, although it might also be a propensity to talk exceedingly rapidly. Even if a child has a great and healthy affection for their cuddly toys, a great and balanced enjoyment of their food, and a balanced relationship with screens, a control pattern may have developed in the child if the child desperately seeks these out as a way of shutting down their vulnerable feelings and blocking their cries.

If a parent has a tendency to dismiss, distract, or reason their child out of expressing their upset feelings, the child may display more surface defensive emotions such as anger and defiance, but will be less likely to express their sadness, grief, disappointments, and fears on a more sustained basis. The youngster learns to seek 'comfort' from the same sources as his or her parents out of desperation, yet the tensions linger under the surface and will soon come to the surface once more.

It is beneficial to your child's emotional well-being to establish a culture of emotional safety between you and them in order to encourage them to open up and slowly begin to address whatever control patterns they may have acquired.

Chapter 10:

Growing With Your Child

When your children are newborns, you place a great deal of emphasis on developmental milestones.

Are they on their feet yet? Do you use whole sentences when you speak? Do you need to go to the bathroom?

After the toddler years are passed, you may stop keeping track of milestones. Unfortunately, many people do not continue to make changes in their parenting practices.

Suddenly, you're engaged in heated debates with your elementary school-aged child, and you're perplexed as to why things aren't functioning the way they used to.

It would be ideal if you could just choose a parenting style and stick with it until your children reach the age of 18.

Unfortunately, as your children develop, your approach to parenting must evolve as well.

Some families slip into behaviors that preserve the kid as a 'baby' even after they have reached the age of twelve! Growing up, it's important to set the bar for what you expect of your children. Take a look at chores, bedtimes, curfews, schoolwork, and even the smallest details like tying the shoes of your 2nd grader or packing the lunch of your middle school student. Because your children are a year older than they were last year, think about how you may adjust the routine, delegate responsibilities, and raise the bar for what is (age-appropriately) required of them this year.

Experiencing Strong Emotions: As your children develop, the method you discuss strong emotions should evolve as well. When it comes to toddlers, we do a lot of the talking for them, such as saying, "Lily took your truck, you're upset." As your kid matures, you may begin to have more open discussions with him or her. Talk to them about what occurred, how the other person may have felt, and how you are feeling in an age-appropriate manner. You should listen more than you speak. Work with your group to analyze what led you to make a poor decision and come up with ideas on how you may do things better in the future.

Allowing your children to experiment with new things is also an important aspect of growing up. The idea of giving their kid greater independence might be frightening for some parents since it involves taking chances. Their child can get injured or fail, or they might make a stupid decision with negative effects. Giving your child the opportunity to attempt new things on their own may, on the other hand, help to boost their confidence and provide them with the opportunity to put into practice the skills you taught them when they were younger. Every child is unique;

some are ready to take on the world straight on, but others must first exhibit their abilities before they can go it alone in their endeavors.

It's easy to keep repeating "I'll tell you when you're older," but before you know it, your child is 'older' and you haven't had a chat with him or her. Rather of having a LARGE TALK about your family values when your children are teenagers, start talking about them while they are little. Start with the most fundamental knowledge possible then add to it over time. Even if the facts you give with your children will differ from one to the next, it is more crucial to maintain the dialogue impartial and open so that your child will feel comfortable asking questions in the future.

Growing up Together. Parenting is a journey and this section focuses on how you grow with the child and the evolution of a parental relationship through patient parenting.

Boundaries will Change. It's also important to know that as you and your child both get older that boundaries will shift and how to adapt to a boundary shift. Something that worked for a three year old won't necessarily work for a thirteen year old.

Setting Expectations for Your Child

Your child is a person in his or her own right.

Examine your own child's strengths and weaknesses, as well as his or her hobbies and abilities. Set your expectations based on the person you are dealing with. Despite the fact that there are numerous charts and averages, statistics, and data available to tell you what the average child at a certain age should be able to perform, no child is just average in any way.

Every child is an individual.

Most children do not fit neatly into any predetermined mold, and their individual skills should be taken into consideration when establishing high expectations for them. Remember to keep in mind that your child is one-of-a-kind while considering developmental standards along the road.

Because I have children from three different sets of parents living in my house, I've had to learn this the difficult way. My previous thought process was that if you parent all of your children in the same way, they would all be pretty much the same. Well, I can now state categorically that this is not the case! What you do as a parent, your personality, your environment, and nature all have a role in how your child performs and what talents and flaws he will have. It is critical to be conscious of and sensitive to this.

Don't base your expectations on your own performance.

Because you may have struggled with arithmetic as a youngster, you may unconsciously anticipate your child to struggle with it as well. Your youngster will, without a doubt, meet and exceed your expectations. This is directly related to the concept of treating your child as an individual. It is critical to avoid having unrealistically low expectations for yourself merely because something was tough for you as a youngster.

Make your points clearly and consistently.

Make it clear what you expect in the long run and identify specific milestones along the route. Demonstrate to your youngster what is expected of him or her in the future. Perhaps attending college is a long-term goal, but make sure to break down the long-term objective into smaller, more manageable chunks along the road. For example, make an effort to keep excellent marks and finish homework assignments on a regular basis. Celebrate your child's short-term victories and enable him or her to bask in the glory of their accomplishments. They will discover that they are capable of exceeding the goals and objectives that have been established for them.

In the event that cleaning a room before going on to playing with stuff in another room is your 'norm,' make certain that it is something that is obviously tied to the previous activity. Also, make an effort to be as consistent as possible with your expectations. Every day, thousands of misunderstandings arise simply because we do not communicate well. This is something I see not only in my relationship with my children, but it also comes into play in my relationship with my spouse.

Remove the all-or-nothing mentality from your life.

While it is necessary to have high expectations for your child, it is also important to communicate to him that falling a bit short of those standards does not imply that he is a failure. You may still make significant progress even if you don't quite meet your lofty expectations when you aim for the highest possible quality. Our tendency for perfection may quickly become habitual if we do not learn to enjoy and embrace the process of progressing toward our goals.

The effort that was done in the process of achieving those standards is worthwhile in and of itself. Rather than broad praise such as "good work," congratulate your child for his or her efforts and successes along the way, focusing on particular features that you see along the route rather than general praise such as "good job." Instead, commend them when they have gone the additional mile to accomplish a task well or when they have utilized problem-solving abilities to correct their own mistakes.

Parents who establish high expectations for their children, explain those goals clearly, and encourage their children to strive for those standards along the way are doing a wonderful service for their children.

Their children learn that they are capable of more than they may believe, that hard effort pays off, and that they are loved regardless of their actions.

Conclusion

Everyone is aware of how difficult it can be to communicate with teens. They roll their eyes, they exhibit disdain, and occasionally they just nod their heads in the hope that you'll finish speaking and they can go on with their lives if only you'd stop talking. Let's face it: when it comes to listening to grownups, teens seem to have a switch that they can toggle on and off. When they desire something or believe that what is being discussed is significant to them, they are receptive and may even appear reasonable to the other person. If it's something they're not interested in, they shouldn't bother with it. You're left with a stonewalling, irritable adolescent who is only interested in getting away from you for the time being.

It is in this context that understanding how to relate to teens might be one of the most valuable lessons an adult can acquire. You just as well be yelling it into an empty field if you have the most brilliant message to deliver to a group of teenagers. After all, it doesn't matter how insightful your message is if they aren't interested in hearing it. Your message will only be effective if it can be shared by both adults and teenagers on a level playing field.

In order to have a productive discussion, consider the following suggestions:

Wait for the appropriate time to strike. When a teenager is unhappy about something or annoyed by a circumstance, it is doubtful that he or she would listen to our point of view on the matter. They might get so preoccupied with their own problems that they are only able to pay attention to their own demands. It is likely that everything we say will be met with deaf ears if this is the case. If we want our communication to be effective, it's critical that the youngster be in a position to hear what we have to say.

Maintain a non-reactive frame of mind yourself. We are all aware of how simple it is to get reactive when teenagers begin to become louder and more belligerent in a scenario with which we are familiar. As they raise their voices, we are more likely to raise ours as well. If we remain cool and non-emotional, the greater the likelihood that the issue will not escalate and that the dialogue will have a more pleasant ending.

If you want to be respected, you must first show respect to others. Teenagers are accustomed to adults acting in a domineering manner. When we were teens, how many times did we get the impression that our thoughts were not valued or that our voices were not heard? As long as we communicate our respect for the teenager, it will be a lot simpler for us to express ourselves and have our opinions taken into consideration.

To be more effective, it is necessary to leave judgment at the door. Teenagers are extremely self-conscious about being evaluated. They've spent their whole childhoods being told what to do and when to do it, as well as feeling judged and scolded by their parents and other adults. When we express our displeasure with a teenager's actions, they may feel overwhelmed and lose their ability to hear us. They may feel defensive and begin to rationalize their actions rather than listening to what we are trying to say.

Pay attention to their issues. We are much too frequently preoccupied in getting our point through that we fail to consider the adolescent's point of view. However, if they feel that they have been heard and that they are being treated with respect, they may be more willing to accept the rules and boundaries that we have established for them.

Define the bounds of acceptable behavior. In order to address expectations inside the house or workplace with a teenager who is in a good mood and not reactive, it is necessary to first establish what is expected of them. Adolescents who are aware about their own boundaries as well as the expectations of the adults with whom they are interacting are less likely to have an out-of-control emotional response.

Maintain focus on the message. Teenagers who don't want to obey rules or who hear anything they are opposed to what they want to hear at the time will frequently attempt to shift the topic. When others disagree with you, they may defend their position by raising their voices in an attempt to gain what they want. The greater the number of adults who can maintain their composure and clarity in their communication, the less likely it is that things will spiral out of control.

While dealing with the fury of a teenager who is not receiving what he or she wants is never easy, being able to maintain your composure under pressure and communicate more effectively is a great step in the right way. Even when they are furious or under stress, teenagers who have well defined boundaries of conduct that have been created as they develop are more likely to stick to these boundaries. Increased effectiveness in communicating with teens increases the likelihood that their interactions will result in favorable consequences for both adults and teenagers.

References

American Psychological Association. (2005). Controlling Anger — Before It Controls You. *Https://Www.apa.org.* https://www.apa.org/topics/anger/control

American Psychological Association. (2021). *How to recognize and deal with anger.* Apa.org. https://www.apa.org/topics/anger/recognize

CABA. (2020, February 3). *Understanding the pressures children and teenagers face.* CABA - the Charity Supporting Chartered Accountants' Wellbeing. https://www.caba.org.uk/help-and-guides/information/understanding-pressures-children-and-teenagers-face

Calm Moment. (2021). *Am I empathetic? Take our quiz to find out how well you relate to other people.* Calm Moment. https://www.calmmoment.com/wellbeing/am-i-empathetic-take-our-quiz-to-find-out-how-well-you-relate-to-other-people/

Consulting.com. (2021). *22 Simple Yet Effective Ways To Be More Patient.* Www.consulting.com. https://www.consulting.com/how-to-be-more-patient

Cross, Dr. G. (2016, March 4). *Parenting With Patience.* HuffPost. https://www.huffpost.com/entry/parenting-with-patience_b_9380880

Family Doctor. (2018, April 16). *Understanding Your Teen's Emotional Health - familydoctor.org.* Familydoctor.org. https://familydoctor.org/understanding-your-teens-emotional-health/

Gelb, S. (2019, June 27). *10 Ways to Become the Parent Your Children Really Need.* Psychology Today. https://www.psychologytoday.com/us/blog/all-grown/201906/10-ways-become-the-parent-your-children-really-need

Gordon, S. (2021, July 26). *Everything Your Teen Needs to Know About Setting Boundaries.* Verywell Family. https://www.verywellfamily.com/boundaries-what-every-teen-needs-to-know-5119428

Lerner, C. (2016, February 29). *Managing Your Own Emotions: The Key to Positive, Effective Parenting.* ZERO to THREE.

https://www.zerotothree.org/resources/338-managing-your-own-emotions-the-key-to-positive-effective-parenting

Mayo Clinic. (2017). *Anger management - Mayo Clinic.* Mayoclinic.org. https://www.mayoclinic.org/tests-procedures/anger-management/about/pac-20385186

Miller, C. C. (2020). How to Be More Empathetic. *The New York Times.* https://www.nytimes.com/guides/year-of-living-better/how-to-be-more-empathetic

Myers, R. (2021). *A Quick Guide To Understanding Your Child.* Child Development Institute. https://childdevelopmentinfo.com/child-development/understanding-your-child-guide/#gs.i7c3m7

Newman, K. (2016, April 5). *The Benefits of Being a Patient Person - Mindful.* Mindful. https://www.mindful.org/the-benefits-of-being-a-patient-person/

Pincus, D. (2021). *Difficult Child Behavior: 4 Tools to Help You Stay Calm.* Empowering Parents. https://www.empoweringparents.com/article/4-

tools-to-help-you-stay-calm-with-your-difficult-child/

Rowden, D. (2021). *How to Be a More Patient Parent | Tips on Parenting Patience*. Empowering Parents. https://www.empoweringparents.com/article/4-steps-to-more-patience-as-a-parent/

Schwartz, D. (2020, February 27). *7 Ways to Get Teenagers to Actually Listen to You | Psychology Today*. Www.psychologytoday.com. https://www.psychologytoday.com/us/blog/adolescents-explained/202002/7-ways-get-teenagers-actually-listen-you

Shaw, B. (2013, August 28). *5 Yoga and Breathing Tips to Conquer Anger Issues*. Parade: Entertainment, Recipes, Health, Life, Holidays. https://parade.com/149706/bethshaw/5-yoga-and-breathing-tips-to-conquer-anger-issues/

Simperingham, G. (2013, April 27). *The Way of the Peaceful Parent*. The Way of the Peaceful Parent. https://www.peacefulparent.com/does-your-child-feel-emotionally-safe-at-home/

Slumberkins, C. (2020, July 9). *Helping Children Feel Safe & Secure*. Slumberkins. https://slumberkins.com/blogs/slumberkins-blog/helping-children-feel-safe-secure

Sturiale, J. (2015, October 14). *Stop Yelling At Your Kids*. WebMD. https://www.webmd.com/parenting/features/stop-yelling-at-your-kids#1

TIMES. (2021, April 19). *How to handle the situation*. The Times of India. https://timesofindia.indiatimes.com/life-style/parenting/toddler-year-and-beyond/how-to-identify-and-handle-an-attention-seeking-child/photostory/82140639.cms?picid=82140985

Printed in Great Britain
by Amazon

76116683R00092